THE BUDDING ENTREPRENEUR

THE BUDDING ENTREPRENEUR

How Young Entrepreneurs and Changemakers Overcome Obstacles to Make an Impact on the World

Aarav Gupta

NEW DEGREE PRESS
COPYRIGHT © 2021 AARAV GUPTA
All rights reserved.

THE BUDDING ENTREPRENEUR
How Young Entrepreneurs and Changemakers Overcome Obstacles to Make an Impact on the World

ISBN
978-1-63676-354-5 *Paperback*
978-1-63676-447-4 *Kindle Ebook*
978-1-63676-356-9 *Digital Ebook*

To Mee Mama, who has taught me so much about entrepreneurship, resilience, and living life to the fullest.

CONTENTS

	INTRODUCTION	9
PART 1	**MENTALITY**	**17**
CHAPTER 1	DOUBT	19
CHAPTER 2	BAD THINGS WILL HAPPEN	41
CHAPTER 3	FAILURE IS NOT A TOTAL FAIL	57
PART 2	**HABITS**	**73**
CHAPTER 4	TRY NEW THINGS	75
CHAPTER 5	POWER OF PURPOSE	89
CHAPTER 6	ALWAYS LEARN	105
PART 3	**GO TIME**	**119**
CHAPTER 7	TAKING ACTION AND EXECUTING	121
CHAPTER 8	THE BEST TIME TO START IS NOW	137
CHAPTER 9	THE IMPORTANCE OF COMMUNITY	151
	CONCLUSION	165
	ACKNOWLEDGMENTS	169
	APPENDIX	171

INTRODUCTION

On March 12, 2020, the principal's voice echoed in the hallways of my school just as I was leaving class: "Attention! Due to the COVID-19 pandemic, school and all school-affiliated activities will be virtual for the next four weeks. Please gather your belongings and exit the building as soon as possible. You and your parents will receive more information regarding the closure via email."

You and I both know that this closure lasted far more than four weeks, but I digress. As promised, school was being taught virtually. The schedule went something like this: teachers would post assignments, students would do them, and our work would be graded. This schedule was repeated every day. To be honest, my workload substantially decreased; it was cut in half!

What would I do with all of this extra time? I spent so much time on TikTok—a short-form, video-sharing app that allows users to create and share fifteen-second videos. I would sing the trending songs on that app in the shower. It's not weird.

Much to my friends and family's shock, I got bored with it soon enough. I began to explore my other passions, especially entrepreneurship, after seeing business-related videos on TikTok.

As a sixteen-year-old high school student, I started to wonder how young people could be successful in the field of business.

Now, to be clear, I'm not just talking about lemonade stands (even though I was a shrewd *lemon-prenuer*). I'm talking about how high school and college students were able to start multimillion-dollar businesses and nonprofits that changed the world.

In other words, how are these young people able to make such an impact?

Is age really just a number, or is this just a saying?

It seemed like the odds were stacked against young entrepreneurs because they didn't have much experience, money, or connections. Yet, I saw these young entrepreneurs raise millions of dollars, be recognized on national television, and have a profound impact on the world.

Why are some able to do this, and others aren't?

This was the question bouncing off the walls of my brain while I was locked in my house during quarantine. I, too, wanted to be a successful entrepreneur, but that would be difficult if I didn't understand what constituted a successful entrepreneur.

I have always had a passion for business and entrepreneurship. Still, I have faced the same limiting beliefs that many do, which caused me to wonder whether I should start a business now or wait until I am older.

Can I, a teenager, really make a difference in the world, or should I wait until I have a college degree and a stable job? These thoughts, beliefs, and doubts began to hold me back, and I began to wonder what young, successful changemakers were doing that I wasn't.

The information on the internet and from business books was fun to read, but I felt that it didn't apply to me—a teenager who has to balance school, sports, clubs, family, friends, extracurricular activities, and so on.

I couldn't manage to get six hours of sleep; how would I ever manage to run a successful company? Through this frustration, I realized that I am not alone. Many other young individuals face similar circumstances when it comes to time management and limiting beliefs.

Millions of young, aspiring entrepreneurs wonder how they can make it work with everything else already on their plates.

In fact, you are probably one of these people! So, I set out to find out what makes a young, successful entrepreneur. Still, more importantly, I embarked on a journey to find out how these lessons can be applied to my life and, ultimately—yours!

Far too many people believe you can't start a business when you're young.

Many believe you should wait until you are older, with many connections and experiences, and have every detail of the business planned out from day zero before starting a venture.

This mentality is one of the main reasons why young entrepreneurship is on the decline. In fact, the number of entrepreneurs between the ages of twenty and thirty-seven has fallen 27 percent from 1996 to 2018. In addition, 60 percent of people who start a business are between the ages of forty and sixty (Simovic 2021).

Now, by no means am I saying it's unwelcome that people between the ages of forty and sixty are starting businesses. Instead, I am expressing how unfortunate it is that the younger generation tends to stay away from entrepreneurship; solely because of their age.

After much research, I am writing this book to tell you that I disagree with the notion of waiting until you are older to start a business. Especially with the preconception that one's age equates to their ability to "have everything planned out perfectly." Instead, *now* is the perfect time to reach for your goals. Yes, if you jump into something that you are not fully prepared for, you might fail, but that is the value of starting young. If you fail at a young age, you can turn that failure into a learning opportunity that can be applied to your life later on. As a young individual, you have fewer liabilities than you will have in the future, minimizing the effects of failing. The first step you take might not go the exact way you wish, but you will be one step closer to your next success.

Young entrepreneurship is difficult considering all of the challenges and limiting beliefs associated with this practice.

This is exactly why I set out to learn from successful entrepreneurs and changemakers and figure out what they did that contributed to their success.

*

THE JOURNEY OF BRENNAN STARK

When he was a junior in high school, Brennan Stark wanted to start a nonprofit with other high school students in which they would build homes for the homeless population. The problem was neither he nor anyone he knew had any experience creating a nonprofit. And to make matters worse, Brennan had absolutely no background in construction. He talked with a friend of his, and they ended up in Home Depot buying materials in what seemed like an endless quest. They literally played around with mud and other materials in Brennan's backyard until they found a material that a house could be built out of.

After a myriad of trials and errors, Brennan and his partner built a seven hundred square foot, net-zero emission house. They gave this home to a homeless father and son, who still live there today. Brennan learned that you may not know where you are going when you start, but you can learn along the way. Worst-case scenario: you fail—but that failure is a learning opportunity. This mentality allowed Brennan to have a powerful impact on the world, but more importantly, it provided a homeless father and son with a house for the rest of their lives.

I wrote this book because I wanted to learn.

The reality is I have gained so much knowledge and understood many topics through this experience—knowledge that I want to share with the public. I have personally interviewed successful entrepreneurs and influential changemakers to learn about their traits and mentalities. I didn't see a reason to learn all of this and then not share it with anyone else.

As a result, I have written what I have learned and packaged it into this book, which will help people following a similar journey.

Perfection is the enemy of progress; thus, waiting for the perfect moment and planning everything out to the T could be what stops you from reaching your full potential. What will happen if you embark on a journey to follow your dreams and you fail?

As daunting as the word "fail" may be, it needs to be rebranded to the word "learn."

If you fail, you can learn what you did wrong, and you will understand what to do and what to avoid the next time around. So is it really a failure? Norman Vincent Peale once said, "Shoot for the moon. Even if you miss, you'll land among the stars."

While the lessons outlined in this book can indeed be applied to anyone of any age, they are *most* applicable to those in school (middle school, high school, college, graduate school, and so on) as well as those who have just finished school and are looking to make a name for themselves in this complicated world. Lastly, this book would be perfect for anyone who faces limiting beliefs (internal or external) due to their age.

Despite your self-doubt, now is the perfect time to chase your dreams because the longer you wait, the fewer opportunities you might have. You can think and plan all day, but nothing will become a reality. until you execute and take action. It might sound harsh, but it's the truth. We will be talking about trying new things, always learning, being prepared for setbacks (and rebounding), dealing with criticism, and much more. You probably picked up this book because you are at least somewhat interested in being an entrepreneur or making a change in the world.

Well, what are you waiting for?

Flip the page, and let's make a change in the world!

PART 1

MENTALITY

1

DOUBT

"Whether you think you can, or you think you can't—you're right."

—HENRY FORD

Picture this:

You are preparing for a presentation at work or school, but you are nervous because you hate public speaking and have little experience. You are not alone—public speaking is the biggest fear ahead of heights, drowning, and zombies (Ingraham 2014). You have to nail this presentation and begin searching for someone who could help you prepare and effectively deliver your message.

You have two options:

1. A forty-year-old cooperate executive

2. A nineteen-year-old college student

Who do you pick to help you?

Now, I'm no magician, but I'm betting you chose the forty-year-old executive. To be honest, I would have picked her as well. In all fairness, she probably has more experience in presentations. She likely knows more about public speaking and has learned many life lessons along the way.

It's natural for society to have more trust in the older generations because they have more life experiences, and they are less likely to make catastrophic mistakes as opposed to someone new to this world.

For young entrepreneurs, changemakers, and anyone looking to make a difference in the world, this is an unfortunate reality. Now, by no means am I saying that older generations have it easier—there is a slew of issues with age discrimination—instead, what I am saying is that far too often, society sees young individuals as inexperienced, unqualified, and sometimes foolish.

This was no exception for Tayo Rockson.

*

TAYO ROCKSON—INTERNAL DOUBT
Born in Nigeria and raised in five different countries, Tayo Rockson was not your everyday kid. From a young age, Tayo faced an identity crisis and did not know who he was or where he could call home. In a French-speaking country, he was a skinny Nigerian kid with a thick accent; in the American school system, he was an awkward child going through puberty. Tayo was seen as different, and his classmates would

mock his accent, crack jokes about his hair, and make fun of his food. The only thing young Tayo wanted to do was fit in and have a place he could call home.

When he would go back to Nigeria, his family would ask, "Are you really Nigerian?" since he had lived in so many different countries. These external doubts about his identity brought a level of insecurity to his life—and he felt like he did not belong to any culture or society.

His Nigerian family did not see him as Nigerian, and his classmates in other countries did not see him as belonging; instead, they saw him as "different."

This identity crisis he faced would soon become the basis for the impact and change he brought to the world.

When Tayo graduated high school, he decided to go to college in Virginia. Socially, he knew it would be difficult because he was a cross-culture kid with no definitive identity. Before he came to the US, he decided he was going to accept himself for who he was, no matter what. He knew that the insults and hurtful comments people made about him would be easier to ignore if he accomplished this. However, self-confidence like this is difficult to achieve.

Tayo explains, "Everybody wants to be seen, heard, and understood for who they really are: rich, poor, middle class, gay, straight, whoever you are." However, "People sometimes lose themselves and they decide [that they are] going to be what [their] parents told [them], or [they are] going to be what society deems to be beautiful this way."

Society often puts people into boxes. Tayo recognized this because it was the primary reason for his identity crisis. He did not let this hold him back. Instead, he used it as motivation to make a positive impact through identity and diversity. However, this was no easy task.

He applied to over eighty-five jobs that would help him make an impact, but all of them turned him down.

He was forced to take any job he was offered so that he could get a visa to stay in the country, even though it did not align with his skill set, desires, or mission.

But one day, his mentality completely changed.

It was August 22, 2012.

Tayo had graduated from college the previous year and was living in Virginia. On what seemed like a typical day, Tayo was driving his burgundy-colored Camry over a bridge on the part of the road that merged onto the highway. He was cruising down his lane at sixty miles an hour, just like he was supposed to.

All of a sudden, the car beside him lost complete control and began spinning erratically. Tayo started swerving to avoid getting hit, but he eventually smashed into the left guard rail. Upon impact, the car lifted up over the guard rail, and Tayo was sure he would flip over the bridge.

"I was certain I was about to meet my end at the age of twenty-two," explains Tayo, but only one thought came to his mind.

"Have you done everything that you said you were going to do?"

He had promised himself he was going to make an impact and help those struggling with identity—but had he done anything?

No, he hadn't.

He was inspired by Nelson Mandela, yet he had not made the impact on the world that he wanted to be remembered for. He was in a town he did not want to be in, he had a job he hated, and he was about to die at the age of twenty-two.

His adrenaline kicked in; he slammed on the brakes and pushed through the car door. Even though his car was totaled, he survived.

"I don't know how I [survived], but I did, and it was my wake-up call," said Tayo.

He wanted to do more with his life.

Shortly after the accident, Tayo quit his job—which was a risky move for an immigrant. To stay in the country, he either had to get married, find a job to sponsor his visa, or go to school. Tayo had just quit his job, finished his school, and had no plans of getting married.

He decided to move to New York City, where he knew no one. He had to find a way to stay in the country, so he enrolled in a Master of Business Administration program. Still, he did not know what to do with his life. He tried anything and everything that came to mind in an attempt to become successful.

He published his blog posts and even started a podcast about identity. He would run around campus and the city itself, looking for people to interview. The podcast allowed Tayo to become a little more confident in what he was doing, but he still faced a lot of doubt.

Tayo points out that in his Nigerian family, "There are really only four options. Doctor, lawyer, engineer, or failure." Tayo was not a doctor, lawyer, or engineer. So did that make him a failure?

In the eyes of many, maybe. But still, he tried to move past those doubts. "There's something about almost losing your life that you say screw it," said Tayo. "I don't care, as long as I'm doing what I want to do, wherever that takes me. I'm fine with it. I just don't want to be a prisoner to someone else's world."

His parents were nervous about his future, and his classmates and colleagues "thought that [Tayo] was bonkers."

People won't see your vision at first, and they may even criticize you, but what is essential is that *you* believe in it and continue to move forward. Tayo always looked at Nelson Mandela as a source of inspiration. Tayo realized that if Mandela spent twenty-seven years in prison and was still able to make an impact on the world, Tayo would be able to change the world as well, no matter how many people doubted him. People continued to contest his podcast and question its validity, but Tayo kept pushing forward. Slowly but surely, his podcast started garnering attention.

Since his podcast covered the stories of third-culture kids, people from all over the world started to send emails to Tayo saying, "I didn't know other people like me existed." People from all age-groups contacted him. They told him stories of how they resonated with him; they were depressed and felt lost, not knowing who they were. They thanked Tayo for making them feel better through the stories he told. The feedback gave him the confidence to stick with the podcast, even though no one knew if it would be profitable. He knew he was making an impact, and it was helping those in need. Thus, he was able to drown out the doubt and insults that people threw his way.

More and more people began to listen to his podcast, and he started to get invited to speak at events. This gave him the confidence to help others by learning about consulting and eventually becoming one. Currently, Tayo is the CEO and president of UYD Management, a consulting firm that helps companies incorporate diversity, inclusion, and social justice. He is also a writer, speaker, consultant, professor, and author of *Use Your Difference to Make a Difference.* In the future, Tayo hopes to continue impacting industries such as the workplace, education, and media by spreading awareness about identity and diversity. Tayo explains the importance of finding yourself and using your identity to your advantage: "One journey that you always have to take is the journey of knowing who you are and what you want to do."

Tayo makes it clear that understanding who you are and believing in yourself is essential when it comes to overcoming the doubts and pressures society puts on you. And while I could not agree more, this can sometimes be difficult considering how we as a society tend to focus on our negative attributes/actions as opposed to our positive ones. This is often called the "negativity bias."

In fact, social scientists have proven that, on average, it takes five pieces of compliments to make up for one piece of criticism (Warrell 2017). In other words, we place five times as much emphasis on criticism than compliments, showing how our brains react more intensely to negativity as compared to positivity.

This idea can be seen in an experiment conducted by Dr. John Cacioppo of Ohio State University (Marano 2003). In this study, participants were shown images classified under three categories: positive (such as pizza, Ferrari, etc.), negative (such as a dead cat), and neutral (such as a plate, hairdryer, etc.). Dr. Cacioppo measured the electrical activity in the brain to see which images the participants reacted to the most. Turns out that there were high levels of brain activity when the negative images were shown. In other words, the participants had more of a reaction when they were shown a negative image as compared to when they were shown a positive image.

I know. I know. You are probably wondering why we are talking about the brain in a book about entrepreneurship. The fact that we tend to focus more on negativity is relevant to our lives since optimism and confidence are critical when it comes to success. I am not saying you should expect to win a billion dollars tomorrow. Instead, I am encouraging you to have hope, as pessimism can hinder your ability to move forward in life.

Psychologist Susan Segerstrom found that ten years after graduating from law school, those who were optimistic made an average of $32,667 more than their pessimistic counterparts (Warrell 2017). Furthermore, Barrie Davenport—a bestselling author—explains, "One of the main obstacles to financial success is low self-confidence [because it] makes us doubt our abilities and judgment and prevents us from taking calculated risks, setting ambitious goals, and acting on them" (Alton 2017).

While I wish I could, I cannot give you a magic potion that will force you to believe in yourself. However, when it comes to particular projects, ventures, or goals, celebrating the little milestones is *key*. In our day and age, it is easy to achieve something, cross it off a list, and move onto the next task, but by doing this, you never have a sense of accomplishment. It is much more beneficial to create smaller, intermediate goals. When you achieve those, you get a boost of confidence, propelling you toward the next milestone.

Writing this book was no easy feat. Not only did it take a great deal of time, but mentally I faced doubts. Will I ever finish the book? Is my writing good enough? Will people read it? Although it was challenging to drown these thoughts out, setting smaller milestones allowed me to push myself toward the intermediate goals. After that, I had more confidence that this endeavor was for me.

For example, I would celebrate when I wrote five thousand words, then ten thousand words, then twenty thousand words, and so on. Your goals and endeavors are marathons, not sprints, and if you treat them like the latter, you will get tired much quicker.

Self-doubt is sometimes inevitable, but it is paramount to recognize it within yourself whenever possible so that it does not hinder your progress and prevent you from reaching your full potential. While self-doubt is obviously a challenge when it comes to entrepreneurship, external doubt can be—and often is—difficult to deal with.

We saw earlier how Tayo Rockson dealt with the doubt he faced by understanding himself and what he was capable of. Tatarit Yensuang took a slightly different approach to deal with age stereotypes, but he embodied some of what Tayo outlined.

*

TATARIT YENSUANG—EXTERNAL DOUBT
Tatarit Yensuang grew up in Thailand. According to him, he "had a pretty average childhood." He was not interested in business, finance, economics, entrepreneurship, or anything related to that realm as a child.

He became interested in technology when he was in elementary and middle school but noted that "none of that translated into the business side of things." He started to explore the different aspects of the tech world that intrigued him, setting the foundation for his future.

Fast-forward a handful of years to when Tatarit began high school. His love for technology earned him internships at different companies and start-ups. Naturally, as a part of internships, he had to talk to many different business people to learn how the company operated.

Tatarit needed to understand a lot about the world of business. Things like: who the customers were, what they needed, what they wanted—and, for that matter, what the difference between their wants and needs even was. He also had to figure out how the product/platform could make their lives easier. All these things would not be easy.

After immersing himself in the world of business and having countless conversations with entrepreneurs and salespeople, Tatarit started to become interested in business and entrepreneurship. He became fascinated with the intersection between technology and business. He soon landed internships in the field, consulted for other companies, and even worked with a handful of start-ups.

Most people told Tatarit, "If you have an interest in business and technology, start a tech company!" However, Tatarit had no plans to launch a start-up at such a young age, "My goal initially was just to see where things take me." All this changed in April 2020. Tatarit had just finished twelfth grade when a high school alum approached him and asked him to work together.

Tatarit explains, "He [the high school alum] came to me, and he was like, 'Do you want to work with me on this idea?'" After some conversation between the two, they decided to start Aturi—a platform that aims to bring high-quality education to students in Thailand and Southeast Asia at a low cost.

These two bright individuals jumped right into establishing this platform. Tatarit conducted customer research as well as interviews to learn what features they should integrate into the platform. As the development process proceeded, Tatarit and his cofounder realized they needed a team of engineers to take their platform to the next level.

Due to the COVID-19 pandemic, all of the interviews for engineers were conducted via Zoom, a popular video-conferencing platform. "We'd invite them onto the call, and they would be a little surprised when they saw a young face," explained Tatarit. The engineers expected to be interviewed by someone older or, at least, the same age as they were. They were wrong. These engineers were interviewed by someone fresh out of high school. Whenever Tatarit asked a question, many of them would often chuckle and respond in a condescending tone because they felt that the founders were too young to be conducting an interview and did not have the authority to ask professional engineers such things. By the engineers' facial expressions, Tatarit could tell they doubted him and his company.

Eventually, they managed to hire some engineers, but that did not mark the end of the skepticism Tatarit faced. Leading a team of engineers was difficult for Tatarit because he was much younger than them. During our interview, Tatarit explained, "There was some awkwardness and some tension because they [the engineers] knew that I was still young—like ten years younger than them." Many of them wondered "Who is this kid, and why is he telling me what to do?" This bothered Tatarit, but it was difficult for him to confront the engineers and change their behavior. Tatarit, as a respectful young man, did not want to offend anyone or disrespect those who were older than him. That being said, he strived to lead the team properly and make sure the company succeeded.

Tatarit showed the engineers that he could find customers, talk to them, and sell their products. He also made it clear that he had development experience from his previous internships and comprehensively displayed his valuable skills to the rest of the team. "As time went on [the relationship with the rest of the team] was something that became easier," Tatarit pointed out.

Tatarit made an interesting point when he said that not all adults were dubious because of his age. Some of them definitely did doubt him and felt he was taking on a role that was too big for him, but many adults actually supported him and offered him guidance. This young entrepreneur spells out the importance of finding people who support you.

In movies and TV shows, entrepreneurship is often portrayed as someone who locks themselves in their room for a month and comes out with a miraculous business. This could not be further from the truth. In reality, entrepreneurship and change-making are about finding a network of people who will support you and be there for you every step of the way. For example, Tatarit found people, like his parents, who offered him advice and guidance. This network of supporters will help you combat the problems you face along the way, such as being doubted by others due to your age. Again, finding people who are willing to be by your side is not an easy task, but I recommend starting with your family and friends and seeing where that takes you.

Through his life experiences (though he has not even lived two decades yet), Tatarit understands that people will doubt him due to his adolescence—it's natural. But at the same time, he has learned the importance of changing the minds of skeptics by letting his work and abilities speak for him.

Tatarit is currently a college student at the University of California, Berkeley, where he continues to explore his passions of technology and business. In the future, this ambitious individual hopes to take Aturi to the next level and change the education industry for the better. He is also interested in learning more about venture capital and how he can get involved in that sphere.

Tatarit learned to deal with external doubt by not only proving what he was capable of and what talents he had, but by finding people who supported him. People will doubt you, but remember, people will support you as well. It is going to be natural to focus on the doubt (negative bias), and it is going to be difficult to try to focus more on the support.

Ben Mathew, another teenage entrepreneur, had a similar story where he faced scrutiny and mockery not only from adults— but also from classmates and people his age.

*

BEN MATHEW—DOUBT FROM EVERY ANGLE

Growing up in central New Jersey, Ben Mathew had a passion for both sports and academics. He enjoyed playing basketball and football, but when he wasn't dribbling down the court or scoring a touchdown, Ben was studying his favorite subject: Math. However, outside of school, Ben quickly fell in love with technology. When his parents first got the iPhone 3G, Ben became addicted. He would play games, see what the camera could do, and explore applications to discover what the device was capable of.

Ben explained, "I remember one time walking into the Apple Store and telling my family I wanted to work at the Genius Bar because I thought it was so cool."

Ben's family would often visit Philadelphia because his grandparents lived there. While in the city, they would swing by to see his father's college friend, who ran his own tech start-up. From a young age, Ben was exposed to both the business and tech side of businesses. He learned about product development, marketing, finances, and other business skills, planting the entrepreneurial seeds in his head.

A few years later, Ben asked his parents for something big. Something that would change their lives forever; something that would influence their future; something that would change the entire family dynamic:

Ben asked for a dog.

Now, this may not seem like a big deal, but those who grew up with parents who did not want dogs are well aware that getting one was a Herculean task. His parents refused, so his best option was to volunteer at an animal shelter. Ben, eager to help the shelter, wanted to raise money for them due to his passion for animals. He baked cookies, sold them to neighbors, and donated the proceeds to the shelter. Over the next five years, Ben donated over $5,000 to the organization. However, Ben would not stop at that. He combined his passions for technology with his love for animals and created an app that made it easier for families to adopt pets.

This entire exercise cemented Ben's love for technology and entrepreneurship.

Entering high school, Ben wanted to continue pursuing his love for tech and business. He joined up with some of his classmates to propose the idea of a hackathon to his school. Ben, a freshman, was a part of the team (consisting of three sophomores and a junior) who pitched the idea to the Board of Education. And everything seemed to be going well—until people heard the news that a freshman was leading the project. His classmates were outraged.

Why were they outraged?

Because a freshman, someone new to the school, was leading a significant project. People would send text messages making fun of Ben and saying he was not qualified for the position. He remembered one notable event when a classmate sent a group text message with the logo of the project Ben was trying to start, asking, "Why is this freshman doing this?"

Being a freshman is not easy in itself, but it makes it ten times harder when your classmates and upperclassmen begin to make fun of you for your passions and put you down for doing what you love. I asked Ben how he coped with these insults and hurtful comments, and he responded by saying, "The first time you hear [the insults], it stings, but then it's a matter of knowing your self-worth." He continued to work on the hackathon and secured funding from large corporations, such as MongoDB and Microsoft. By bringing these names to his school, he started to show he was capable of much more than his peers previously thought. This would not be the end of the doubt he faced because of his young age.

People continued to make fun of him and mock him since entrepreneurship was not common in his high school, and what he was doing was "out of the norm." It was also difficult for Ben to see his classmates earning medals and trophies for baseball, cross-country, and lacrosse while he was on the phone with engineers and charities. He did not have a physical award to show for this work—and to make matters worse, he was criticized for the way he spent his time because of his young age.

Through these difficult experiences, Ben learned that "You have to realize that what you are working on is bigger than what other people see." Identifying those who have your back and those who support you, as opposed to those who put you down for following your dreams, is crucial. As difficult as it was, Ben continued to push forward into his next venture.

While volunteering at a soup kitchen, Ben started to realize that there were a lot of inefficiencies when it came to the logistics of people donating food. He saw this as another opportunity to combine his love for tech and his passion for helping others. After talking to numerous app developers and speaking with over thirty charities, Ben launched Dovtail—an online platform that streamed the donation process from individuals to organizations. Now it was time to market the platform.

This was a challenge for Ben because he planned on using social media to spread the word about Dovtail; however, many of his social media connections were students at his high school—the same students who made fun of him about his hackathon idea. A lot of pressure is still being put on students to be "popular" in high school, and Ben felt that his entrepreneurial ventures were not helping his cause. Ben provided some insight into his emotional state at the time, saying, "I would be scared to post on Instagram that I am launching Dovtail because I know what people have said behind my back. I know what people have said to my face." At this point, most high school students would throw their hands up and give in to the social norm of not pursuing entrepreneurship at their young age.

But as you probably figured out by now, Ben is not like most high school students. Ben marketed his platform in every way possible despite the previous insults he endured. He pushed through his mental roadblock because he knew people would eventually take him seriously if he showed what he was capable of. Ben stated, "Once you do it [the act of following your dreams] constantly, and you do it well, that becomes a part of your reputation." Ben saw initial success with the platform and hoped to expand. Now, if this was a fairy tale, Ben would have expanded across the country and would never face age discrimination ever again. Unfortunately, that wasn't the case.

When Ben was visiting Austin, Texas, he stopped at a shelter to see if they would use his platform, Dovtail. He set up a meeting with the head of the shelter, and when Ben arrived, they looked at the teenager and "you could tell from his facial expression that he was not expecting a seventeen-year-old to walk in." The head realized Ben was "just" a teenager and assumed he had nothing valuable to offer. The head said, "I only have twenty minutes for you." Ben was trying to make every minute count as he pitched his platform and showed its existing impact on his community and other shelters worldwide.

The meeting lasted ninety minutes—and the shelter ended up joining Dovtail. Ben realized that people will doubt him because of his age. But, as evidenced by his experience with his hackathon idea, he learned that if you perform and show what value you add, people will begin to believe in you. In other words, let your work speak for you and show the world what you have.

Ben's advice for overcoming ageism is to not be shy, publicize your accomplishments, and understand why people make fun of you and doubt your abilities. Obviously, being outgoing is easier said than done. Still, it is paramount to be proud of what you are doing instead of being ashamed of it. Ben does not want to look back on his life and regret not doing something. I don't either, and I bet you don't as well. He would regret not creating Dovtail, which is why he is happy he embarked on that journey despite all the insults hurled at him.

Ben pointed out, "It's a matter of just trying something because you don't know what's going to happen with it."

Most people understand the importance of marketing something before its release, but it is just as important to talk about it afterward because it shows how successful and impactful it was. On social media, Ben would post something along the lines of: "We have seen two hundred students come through, $15,000 in funding, and speakers from many companies." Ben pointed out, "When people see those numbers, they're like 'Damn, this kid's actually doing something, and it's not just all talk.'"

*

TAKEAWAY

Entrepreneurship in high school is not what people usually do—and because it is different, some people will make fun of you. This may sound crazy, but try to *understand* why people are making fun of you and mocking what you are doing. People may try to put you down since they envy how much courage you have for taking on such projects at a young age. As cliché as it might sound, you have to realize that what you are doing is worth doing, no matter what others say.

You will face insults, criticisms, and hurtful comments from some classmates and adults, but as long as you know that what you are doing will have an impact, those comments will mean nothing.

Whether internally or externally, you probably have faced doubt, and you will experience it again in the future.

However, limiting doubt—not eliminating it entirely—is often beneficial because it allows you to move forward with less hesitation.

And who knows, maybe someday that nervous presenter will pick *you* to be their public speaking coach!

2

BAD THINGS WILL HAPPEN

---

*"It's **not** how **many times you** get knocked down that count, it's how **many times you** get back up."*
—GEORGE A. CUSTER

Imagine you are running a monumental race. This may be a five-kilometer or a full marathon—your choice. At some point during the race, you encounter a twenty-foot-high wall blocking your path and preventing you from moving forward. You don't know where it came from, but it's there! How would you feel? Throwing in the towel and giving up may be on your mind, or maybe you will begin to think of creative ways to tackle this obstacle. Although we don't know too much about this situation—after all, it is hypothetical—we do know one thing for sure: if you give up every time you encounter that wall, you will never reach the end of the race.

Like in a race, the same lesson applies in life, business, and entrepreneurship—that being: grit and perseverance are critical attributes when it comes to success. Angela Duckworth, a psychologist at the University of Pennsylvania and the author of *Grit: The Power of Perseverance and Passion,* defines grit as "perseverance and passion for long-term goals" (Agarwal 2019). Notice the use of the phrase "long-term." Grit does not mean never giving up no matter what, but what it does mean is not giving up on your long-term goals just because you encounter a roadblock.

Take the race scenario as an example again. Say you try to get a running start and run up the wall, defying all gravity and physics. It doesn't work out, but it's okay (and a good idea) to quit doing that and try another method. Maybe you find a rope and try pulling yourself up. You abandoned the "vehicle" you were using to reach your goal, but you never gave up on chasing it.

Entrepreneurs are constantly facing setbacks, but this is not a reason to stop trying. It's not easy, and I won't say that it is, to keep moving forward after fighting so many obstacles. Still, the reality is: obstacles will fall in your way, and you need to embrace them and move past them to succeed. Pivot and try something new if you need to. Bad things will happen, but this will not define you or your journey.

*

BEING KICKED OUT OF YOUR OWN COMPANY
In the summer of 2020, we were all quarantined due to the COVID-19 pandemic. I was a rising junior in high school, and I was really hoping the pandemic would be over by then. As

you all know, I was wrong. I was not able to go on vacation, see my friends, go to camp, walk around town, and so on. I was stuck inside, and I was upset because I felt like my life was restricted and it "wasn't fair." That was wrong and selfish of me. People were suffering in so many ways than I could even imagine. Some were battling to put food on the table, pay their rent, hold onto their job, and many were putting their lives on the line for their community. I felt lucky to have a roof over my head and be healthy while others struggled to make ends meet and live their lives as they deserved to. Yes, the pandemic affected me, but I realized that so many people were hurting more than I was.

I wanted to make an impact and help those who were affected by COVID. After some online research and conversations with others, I started to recognize that many low-income families were struggling with education. Education inequality has always been an issue in society, but the pandemic would only worsen the situation. I saw this as an opportunity where I could help the community and help those in need. I used to tutor a student from a low-income neighborhood, and I came to the realization that there were numerous students in need of educational support, especially during the pandemic.

I came up with the idea to partner high school students with students in low-income areas. They would be tutored in a subject they desired, such as English, Mathematics, Science, History, and so on. All of the sessions would take place virtually via Zoom, and they could be accessed from a phone or a public library. They would be tailored to the student so that they would get the most out of it. There would be no cost for anyone since the high school tutors would volunteer their time out of the goodness of their own hearts. I was really excited to see how this venture would help those in need!

I met another high school student at a virtual entrepreneurship program; and reached out to him to connect and see if we could work on the tutoring idea I had. For privacy purposes, we will call this high school student Rob. After pitching my idea to Rob, he instantly fell in love with it. We decided to become business partners. We spent more hours than I can count talking on the phone, texting each other, and planning the organization via Zoom.

We created a business plan outlining our mission statement and how we could make this idea a reality. Eventually, we created a website that outlined our goal and how we planned on helping those in need. After much discussion of marketing strategies, we launched the platform. I could not tell you how excited I was to see my idea go from a thought in my head to a reality. But more importantly, I was happy to see the limitless opportunities that this platform would provide low-income families with. We marketed the platform to family and friends, and I was able to get dozens of my classmates to sign up to be tutors. The organization began to pick up traction with all of our efforts!

On Tuesday, August 18, I woke up after a tedious night spent working on the platform. I picked up my phone from my white nightstand to check the status of the Instagram account. It would not let me log into the account for some reason. Since I had just woken up, I was groggy, and I was not in the mood to troubleshoot all of these tech issues. So naturally, I closed the app, waited a few minutes, and tried again, but it still would not let me log in. I texted him: "Hey Rob, did you change the Instagram password because it is not letting me in?" I got no response. I initially did not think anything of it—though, eventually, I started to wonder what was happening because it was unusual for Rob to take this long to respond. I tried texting him again, calling him, and even emailing him—but still I heard nothing.

Turns out, he blocked my phone number and blocked me on Instagram. I checked the organization's page on another account and realized that Rob had continued the project without me. He had locked me out of the Instagram account, website, email, and all other outlets. I tried to reach out to him, but to no avail. He shut me out of everything, threw me aside, and continued to work on my idea and the business we started together (all the while posting about the project on the Instagram business account). Why did he throw me aside? Most likely because he wanted to take credit for the entire idea without sharing the spotlight with anyone else. I had trouble accepting this reality because I had spent a great deal of time developing, marketing, and eventually launching this project. I was hurt—and did not realize that a high school student could be this corrupt. I did not know what would happen with the organization now that I was kicked out of it. Would it still help low-income families? Would he stick to the mission statement? Would it still combat the effects of COVID-19? Who knew?

Although I wish I could say I quickly brushed off the dust, got back on my feet, and continued on with my life—the reality is: I had trouble understanding that I would no longer be working in this organization, and it was gone forever. However,

I eventually went back and realized that the central goal of this tutoring program was to help those struggling during the pandemic. I could still make an impact without Rob.

Another idea I had (luckily, I didn't tell Rob about this one) was to create designs, print them on T-shirts, sell said shirts, and then donate the profits to a local hospital to support frontline workers. Millions of people were suffering from the pandemic, and frontline workers were no exception. I partnered with a friend of mine to launch this organization called Frontline Apparel to support frontline workers, but more on that later.

Through these rough experiences, I not only learned the importance of getting a business partnership in writing; but also how setbacks will occur in any path you take in life. These setbacks can sometimes be avoided, but other times they are out of your control. It is essential to learn how to pivot and move on from a failure. However, it can also be exceedingly helpful to comprehend the lessons that such a setback offered you.

Omer Shai, the Chief Marketing Officer for Wix, made an interesting point when he said, "Starting something isn't enough. The ability to persevere and be resilient after that something has been started is the true stamp of an entrepreneur." This goes hand in hand with what Angela Duckworth learned from her personal experiences and research. Duckworth used to be a seventh-grade mathematics teacher. She once noticed that some of her students, who weren't naturally gifted in mathematics, were doing better on tests than the bright students in her class. After digging a little deeper, she understood that the students who did not have a natural talent for math but worked really hard and kept trying, no matter what, scored better on their exams than those who were good at math but did not work hard and were discouraged easily. This encouraged Duckworth to do more research, and she found that talent is not the primary focus of success; rather, perseverance and passion are. Setbacks are common; thus, how one deals with them is crucial for their future endeavors, no matter how much talent they have.

Setbacks come in different forms and are different for everyone. For some, it may be an event that occurred, which created an obstacle. For others, it may be criticism and negative feedback that they received, which discouraged them and forced them to doubt themselves. This is what happened to Ashley Olafsen.

*

CRITICISM

Ashley grew up in Massachusetts, and she explained that her school district was filled with many opportunities and teachers who were willing to support her. She was the eldest of three, and she always engaged in pretend-play with her younger siblings. "This allowed me to practice leadership and explore my creativity at a really young age," Ashley pointed out. Whether she knew it or not, the groundwork for her entrepreneurial endeavors was being set as she played creative games with her family.

In school, Ashley tried a whole bunch of different activities, but she never really felt connected to or enjoyed any of them.

Until she discovered the middle school theater program in seventh grade, that is. It gave her the ability to express herself and "explore different personalities." As a theater kid, Ashley never really had entrepreneurship at the top of her mind. "I wasn't intending to get into entrepreneurship," stated Ashley. Instead, she was inspired to engage in the entrepreneurial field because she "was moved by [her] own passion and by the problems within [her] community."

In high school, she noticed that she and all of her friends were "really struggling with self-esteem and mental health." She wondered why this was not a more common theme for discussions within schools and asked herself, "Why isn't anyone talking about this?" She wanted to host an open conversation and forum to help people understand their self-worth. At the age of sixteen, she got together with some of her friends and decided to hold a workshop at their local middle school for a group of eighth-grade girls about self-esteem, confidence, and mental health. "That was truly supposed to be it," said Ashley. "We weren't planning on doing more workshops. We weren't planning on starting a business." As you may be able to tell by the themes presented in this book, she was wrong.

The first workshop that Ashley and her friends conducted went so well that the school asked them to come back and host two more. At the second workshop, Ashley met an eighth-grade girl who attended that middle school. She was inspired by what Ashley was doing and asked if she could work with her, run a summer program with her, and eventually a company. Ashley said, "Yes, absolutely," and, in fact, they are still best friends today! These two women started MOVE, an organization designed to empower young women and encourage them to reach their true potential.

At their very first MOVE workshop (about a year after Ashley gave her first workshop), Ashley and her cofounder got a complaint from one of the parents. It said that the environment was not comfortable enough. They were "devastated and heartbroken" because all they wanted to do was help others, and now they were getting a complaint saying the environment they created was not comfortable. Ashley explained that they "never wanted to give another workshop again. We felt like we had let ourselves down, the people around us, and the teacher who was helping us. We felt really, really humiliated." However, they had to give the second workshop because they had promised to do so over a month in advance. This was a substantial setback because they felt discouraged and questioned the impact they were really having.

As embarrassing and discouraging as it was, Ashley and her cofounder took the complaint very seriously. They altered numerous aspects of the program so that it was more welcoming, inclusive, and comfortable. They made simple changes, which caused a considerable difference. For example, they would have music playing when people entered the workshop. Also, they had licensed guidance counselors at every workshop in case people wanted to talk to them; and encouraged students to sit near people they did not know, so new bonds could be formed. Moreover, they had icebreakers that united people of all grades, no matter if they were in middle school or high school. "It shaped the rest of the business for years to come," said Ashley when she was describing the parent complaint. "It was very critical feedback that we received." Ashley and her cofounder used this setback to their advantage, which allowed them to help more people and have a more pronounced impact on their community.

Currently, Ashley works at IFundWomen, where she coaches women founders. She hopes to continue doing this in the future because she finds it quite fulfilling.

The resilient mentality that Ashley developed at such a young age has served her well and will continue to help her in the years to come. Research from McGill University found that perseverance, academic success, and real-world success all have a positive relationship (Bazelais, Lemay and Doleck 2017). This should not be a surprise considering that the more we throw in the towel, the less likely we are to achieve success because we have fewer opportunities. In other words, a person who encounters a setback, but continues pushing forward, is more likely to reach their goals compared to someone who gave up after running into their obstacle. Moreover, studies have shown that resilience and optimism are linked with healthier and more fulfilling lifestyles (Ellin 2020). Such a mentality has benefits on both a professional and personal level!

Not being entirely discouraged from a setback (though it's normal to be at least somewhat discouraged) is critical because it not only allows us to keep pushing forward but it also encourages us to pivot and find ways to avoid future obstacles.

*

FRONTLINE APPAREL

As I mentioned earlier, I was kicked out of the tutoring organization that I helped start, but that wouldn't stop me from pursuing another community project. I had just begun my junior year in high school, and I started to see that some frontline workers were struggling financially to make ends meet. I wanted to raise money through T-shirt sales to combat this issue and offer support to those risking their lives for the community. I talked with one of my friends from high school (we will call him Joe for privacy reasons), told him about my idea, and asked if he wanted to work for me. I know what you are thinking: "Isn't this exactly what happened with the tutoring organization? You told someone about your idea; they stole it and executed upon it without you. Why would you do this again?"

These are all valid points. The difference here was that since I already had a terrible experience with the tutoring organization, I knew how to prevent this from happening again in the future. In other words, I had turned my "failure" into a learning opportunity that would allow me to avert the same incident from occurring. After Joe agreed to work with me, we decided we would create separate, mutual accounts (Instagram, Gmail, Facebook, etc.), which we both had access to for the business. We would put all usernames and passwords on a shared document so that neither one of us could be locked out of the business. In the scenario with Rob and the tutoring organization, Rob had too much control because he knew some of the passwords that I did not. I thought this would not be a big deal—but boy, was I wrong.

Now I know better! Joe and I created mutual business accounts with Google, Instagram, Wix, and so on. Together, we drew up fun, creative, and innovative T-shirt designs that related to COVID-19. Then, we created a website with a mission statement, explaining what our goals were and how we would accomplish them. After Joe and I found a manufacturer that could bring our designs to life at an affordable price, we decided what each T-shirt would retail for and added the online store to the website. After this step, I recall telling Joe, "I think this organization is really going to have an impact on the community!" I was excited that we had come this far, and we were ready to launch the organization, which would be called Frontline Apparel.

We did hit a minor roadblock, however. We needed to connect a bank account to the website to launch the organization. This meant that two minors, who were only seventeen years of age, would need to create a bank account. That was going to be difficult. I spoke with my father to see if he would cosign the bank account, and luckily, he agreed. However, we were in the middle of a dangerous pandemic, so it was going to be nearly impossible to walk into the bank and set up the account. We had to do it virtually, which was quite challenging. After dozens of back-and-forth emails, conversations with Joe and my parents, and mailing legal documents back and forth, the bank account was finally set up! I genuinely thought we had overcome this sizable roadblock, and we were ready to launch the organization. Again, I was wrong!

It was 8:00 p.m. on Tuesday, December 22, 2020. I logged onto a Zoom call with Joe to discuss how we were going to move forward with Frontline Apparel. The initial conversation went something like this:

Aarav: "Joe, great news! The bank account is set up, so we are ready to go!"

Joe: "Awesome, the website asks for the bank account number, routing number, and date of birth."

I read all of the information aloud.

Joe: "It says that there is a problem with the birthday."

Aarav: "What do you mean a problem with the birthday? That's my birthday."

Joe: "Ohhhhhh, it says that we need to be over eighteen to proceed."

Aarav: "Uh-oh."

I called my dad into the room and explained what had happened. I asked him if we could use his name as the business owner since he was over eighteen years old. This was when all of our work came crashing down (or so we thought). My dad works on Wall Street, and his compliance team at work stated that neither he nor anyone else in his family can be associated with a business unless they get clearance from the firm. Joe and I needed to register as an organization to launch Frontline Apparel, and we were not going to have the time to get approval since we wanted to rush to market as soon as possible. "I'm not sure that this venture is possible if you have to register as a business or organization," my dad explained. This was going to be a *huge* roadblock. Obviously, we wanted to comply with the rules, and the rules were that we could not start a business.

Something inside Joe and me prompted us to stay on the Zoom call and brainstorm solutions. We accepted the fact that we were not going to be able to start a business and make an impact in that manner, but that didn't mean we could not make an impact another way. Custom Ink allows users to design clothing, set up a fundraiser online, sell apparel, and donate profits to a charity. This would all be possible without setting up a business, and we would be following all of the rules. And that was what we were going to do!

We spent the next twenty-four hours redesigning our entire idea and reworking numerous aspects of Frontline Apparel. It was not easy, but we did not have another choice if we wanted to help our community. We set up the Custom Ink store with all of our designs and apparel that we were planning on selling. Because our focus had shifted, we needed to redesign the website and update it so that it was an accurate depiction of our new goal and what we were currently doing. After researching statistics surrounding COVID-19, Joe and I created a promotional video that would be displayed not only on our website but also on the Custom Ink store.

Since we wanted to maximize impact, we wrote an article advertising the case. We even reached out to our local hospital to find out if we could partner with them, and they agreed! After increasing our social media presence, the marketing process began! Twenty-four hours after hitting a major roadblock, we had already pivoted and taken a slightly different path. But the essential takeaway from this process was that the path we ended up taking still led us to our goal—helping the community and those suffering due to the pandemic.

I cannot say the journey was easy, but after being kicked out of an organization that I conceptualized and hitting numerous barriers with Frontline Apparel, we learned the importance of pivoting and being flexible because sometimes things around us do not work out as we wanted them to. Adaptability is vital in a constantly changing world because not everything can be predicted. As Mike Tyson once said, "Everyone has a plan until they get punched in the mouth."

I think it has been made quite clear how powerful grit is—but, believe it or not, this mentality and trait affects more than just yourself. If you are a leader in any capacity, having grit allows you and your team to put their best work forward. According to *Forbes*, a study of five hundred leaders found that the more-resilient leaders scored seventy-five points higher on their leadership effectiveness index compared to their less-resilient counterparts (Folkman 2017). Again, this should not be a surprise. You are inspired by the people around you, and if you are being led by someone who is discouraged easily and gives up often, you will begin to take after them.

*

TAKEAWAY

Being more resilient is not easy, and it takes a lot of practice. You are not going to instantly become more resilient by reading this book; rather, this book offers a few solutions to build this mentality within yourself.

Be optimistic and know that one setback does not define you. Always look for the light at the end of the tunnel, and when something goes wrong, look on the bright side. For example, think about how you got better at dealing with problems and adverse outcomes; and how that made you better prepared for the future. Always know there is a brighter future ahead, and by keeping this in mind, you will be more encouraged to move forward and pursue your dreams. Understand that one obstacle does not define you, and just because you encountered one does not mean you will face them everywhere you turn.

Develop a support network of people who will encourage you. This may be friends, family, or coworkers, but no matter who they are, make sure they are encouraging you to do your best. They won't let you give up just because one thing went wrong—and while this may seem annoying, it is very constructive.

Understand that setbacks are inevitable and bad things will happen. If you are telling yourself success is a straight line and nothing will go wrong—well, you are lying to yourself. The more you believe in this false narrative, the more shocked you will be when you actually encounter a setback. Know that you will face obstacles, but you have the ability to overcome all of them, and you can overcome all of them if you chose. That being said, be optimistic, but also be realistic.

An article from the online publishing platform Medium explains, "Starting a business is like running an obstacle race. It's a never-ending path of obstacles from start to finish" (Gomes 2019). Don't fool yourself by saying everything will run perfectly—because it won't. But with grit, determination, and perseverance, obstacles are just opportunities to learn from.

3

FAILURE IS NOT A TOTAL FAIL

―

"I have not failed. I've just found 10,000 ways that won't work."

—THOMAS A. EDISON

Walt Disney. Ariana Huffington. Michael Bloomberg. What do these three individuals have in common? You could say talent, money, experience—or failure. Yes, you read that right; all three of these powerful and successful individuals have faced failure in their life. Disney was told he had no sense of creativity before he launched the Walt Disney Company. Huffington was rejected by numerous publishers for her second book prior to creating the *Huffington Post*. And Bloomberg started his own company simply because no one would hire him.

Far too often, people view an undesirable outcome in entrepreneurship as a devastating failure they cannot recover from. While this may seem like the case in many situations, in reality, this could not be farther from the truth. Failure is not permanent, and in many ways, it is beneficial because it is a learning opportunity. It is not a waste of time to try something and fail, especially if you learn from experiences and your mistakes.

*

THE FAST-FOOD EXPERIMENT

I had just finished middle school, and it was summertime when my friend and I were playing tennis at our local park. I asked him, "What are you doing over the summer?" He did not have too many concrete plans, and neither did I. Still, we were both interested in business and entrepreneurship and wanted to pursue this passion over the summer. We landed in an entrepreneurship summer school class for high school students and were fortunate enough to have a fantastic professor who spoke about business plans, morality when conducting negotiations, and presenting to investors. One aspect of this program was partnering up, coming up with the business idea, creating a pitch, and presenting it to a panel of experts at the end of the program.

My friend and I partnered up and tried to come up with a lucrative business idea. We spent countless hours talking during the program and in the evening on the phone—and eventually settled on an idea we both loved! Our concept was a fast-food Indian restaurant that would supply high-quality food at an affordable price in sixty seconds or less. We were planning on making all of the food kosher, vegetarian, and less than two dollars. We did some research into this market, purchased a domain for the business, drafted a business plan, calculated expenses, and began working on the presentation (pitch deck). We even created a video showing ourselves making one of the dishes in sixty seconds!

On the day of the presentation, we were definitely nervous, but we knew we put our best work forward and hoped the judges would like the idea and our efforts. The other teams presented their creations, and after some deliberation between the judges, and anxious chatter, it was announced that we won first place! On top of that, after the program concluded, one of the judges came up to us and said, "I was very much impressed with your concept and pitch. I hope that you will execute upon this in the near future." This comment, along with our love for the idea, made us want to continue this endeavor. So we did just that. Correction: we *tried* to do just that.

We realized that renting a space to open a restaurant was a little impractical for two high school freshmen. And not to add insult to injury, but the starting expenses were around $400,000. My math may be wrong, but I didn't think my weekly allowance of $15 would cover that. "What if we make the food at home and deliver it?" We thought. We could use a platform like Grubhub or DoorDash. We actually submitted a request to be listed on Grubhub even though we had nothing set up. Oops. As it turned out, Grubhub didn't list us on their platform, and we began to realize that our idea was not too practical. Making high-quality food and selling it for two dollars left us with pennies on the dollar as profit. Plus, making all the food in sixty seconds would be a challenge.

While we still loved the idea, we started to accept the reality that executing this business plan might not be the smartest move. We ended up moving on from this project and focused on other aspects of our lives.

Our idea did not go as planned. We did not make a splash in the fast-food industry. We did not make large sums of money. We did not even launch the business. But here is what we *did* learn:

- Brainstormed business ideas

- Researched different industries and sectors of the economy to learn about size, trends, customers, and competitors

- Wrote a business plan

- Budgeted the finances

- Determined attractive prices for items on the menu

- Calculated margins and figured out how much we have to sell to stay afloat

- Figured out what we need to do to get the business running

- Discussed marketing tactics

- Thought about how we were going to set ourselves apart from our competitors

- Considered different business models and the economics behind them (for example, a franchise model)

- Came up with an exit plan/how investors are going to get their money back

- Created a compelling presentation

- Conveyed our mission and vision to a panel of experts and judges

- And much more

Now, I don't say any of this to brag. I mean, what is there to brag about? We never even started the business! I say this to show what we gained from this venture.

You may be surprised to learn that 21.5 percent of start-ups fail within their first year. Additionally, 30 percent fail within their second year, 50 percent within their fifth year, and 70 percent within their tenth year (Bryant 2020). The fast-food business that I tried to start failed within the first month. But as I mentioned, it was not really a failure, seeing as we learned a great deal from the journey. As Toni Koraza explained in a Medium article, "Every failure leaves an emotional scar that teaches us valuable lessons" (Koraza 2019). I am not saying you should expect to fail; instead, I am simply pointing out that when you realize that the worst possible outcome (in this case: failure) is not the end of the world, you are more likely to try new things and find success that way.

*

REAL ESTATE MANAGER AT FOURTEEN YEARS OLD

Growing up in Kansas City, Sydney Phillips was not your average child. Though certainly not in a negative way, mind you! But she was different from other kids her age. Instead of asking for Disney princesses and dresses, she asked for suits. Sydney wanted to be a CEO from a young age. In fact, rather than playing dress-up and having tea parties, she would make her parents sit around a table and pretend she was conducting a board meeting. During my interview with Sydney, she admitted, "I was an odd child, to say the least."

When she turned fourteen, she and her family experienced a life-altering, tragic event. Her father had a heart attack and suddenly passed away. She woke up one morning, and her father was gone. Sydney's father had an identical twin brother, and, unfortunately, two months after her father's death, he was diagnosed with stage 4 stomach cancer. The entire family went to the Mayo Clinic to care for the brother, leaving Sydney behind. She was left behind in a house without her family and was expected to run the family real estate business. She was only fourteen years old. This young child felt lost in every way possible. She needed to figure out how to use the washing machine, get to school, earn good grades, and run the family real estate business.

The first year after taking over the business, she lost a great deal of money, and she had trouble balancing her schoolwork with the real estate venture. She convinced her history teacher that she could learn the material on her own; thus, there was no need for her to go to class. During her history period, she would leave the school, go to Barnes and Noble, and read about commercial real estate investing. Sydney thought, "I don't need to know the history of all the presidents right now. I need to make sure that dinner is on my table." She continued to operate the real estate business; and learned two valuable lessons along the way, which would help her for the rest of her life: execution and failure.

Her first lesson was execution. She realized the importance of executing and taking action rather than planning out minor details. Sydney pointed out that too many people have a brilliant idea, but then they just leave it at that. It's not about what idea you have; it's about what you do with those ideas. She offered us the example of Airbnb and how it was a terrible idea. Think about it: you rent a room in your house to a stranger, and you live with them without even knowing what they are like. Despite the terrible idea, Airbnb as a company had flawless execution, which is what made it a billion-dollar company.

Sydney offered some valuable insight, saying, "You give up perfection whenever you start a business [because] finished is better than perfect." When thinking about expanding her real estate business, Sydney was able to put perfectionism aside and realize that she must move forward and execute. She made bold decisions with the business to find success and compete with other companies. It wasn't easy for her to put perfectionism aside, but it was necessary.

Her second lesson was failure. Sydney acknowledged that failure is not easy to overcome; however, it is prudent to be comfortable with it because it is what fuels your success. Sydney described how she surpassed her fear of failure. She visualized her fear as a friend who just wants the best for her.

They may call thirty times a day to ensure she is not setting herself up for failure, and they may even encourage her to quit her goals if they feel she will fail.

She uses this tactic to understand that what she does is not her "friend's" decision. It is Sydney's decision. By making your fear something external rather than internal, you can look at it logically and realize how irrational the thoughts are. When considering taking a risk in her real estate company, she likely feared failing; and wondered what it would mean for the company. She turned this fear outward in the form of an anxious "friend" who was bugging her and was able to see her concerns through an analytical lens. She would see that the fear may be irrational—but even if the fear was valid and she did fail, it would be a learning opportunity.

Everyone fails. Even the most successful people. However, we tend to only hear about their successes. "What you don't hear about is how many failed attempts [they've had]." "Persistence and failure are grossly underestimated," said Sydney. "They say that only 10 percent of the start-ups survive. Okay, that's fine. Go start ten businesses, and one out of the ten is going to work."

Through all the lessons she learned in the first year of being a real estate tycoon, she was able to break even by her second year. "I was like, 'Oh my gosh. I didn't lose money,'" explained Sydney. By the time she was sixteen years old, the business was profitable!

Currently, Sydney is on her eighth business, and she openly admits that three of them have completely failed. With all this success, you might think she left failure behind her. But that couldn't be farther from the truth. Sydney explained that she fails on a weekly basis. Failure greets her in the form of not communicating with her team, falling behind on a project, or missing an opportunity. Sydney stated, "Failure is more temporary than it is a [permanent] defeat," and you should be proud of them instead of hiding them. In fact, the day Sydney was named Young Female Entrepreneur of The Year, one of her businesses was $500 from going under. And guess what? She posted about both events!

Because of all of her failures and lessons learned, Sydney is now an influential commercial real estate investor and developer, a tech founder, founder of an investment ground that supports LGBTQ+ and minority founders, and the host of *The Pink Suit Podcast*. In the future, Sydney hopes to be the first private female space founder to send a mission to Mars and back. She also dreams of having the largest augmented reality company in the world and of starting The Pink Suit Foundation—which will donate suits to young female founders. She always wanted a suit as a child, and now she is returning the favor to others.

Sydney left us with an important message: keep trying new things, starting new ventures, and shooting for the stars because eventually, one of them will succeed. If you are given twenty attempts to throw a basketball in a hoop, the probability of making one is far greater than if you only had a single shot.

*

LESSONS LEARNED FROM AN ONLINE BUSINESS FAILURE

During the summer of 2020, I was thinking about the ways a teenager like myself could make money from home. That's when drop-shipping came to my mind!

In short, drop-shipping is when you set up an online business selling certain goods already being produced and partner with the manufacturer of said goods. When something gets sold on your website, you keep the difference between the sale price and the manufacturer's charge. It sounds pretty simple, and the concept is, but making substantial money through this method can be difficult. Anyway, I decided to start an online business selling kitchen gadgets using this method.

I ordered sample kitchen gadgets ranging from unique pizza cutters and versatile snack bowls to innovative fruit baskets and cool-looking olive oil sprayers. I was sure all of the products were going to be great.

One kitchen gadget I thought would be especially useful was a plastic sealer. This tool would reseal any bag made of plastic (chips, for example), so the food would stay fresh, even after opening the bag. Genius! When the shipment arrived, I swung open the door, grabbed the box, ripped it open, and looked at the plastic sealer.

It was magnificent! I ran to my kitchen with this beauty in my hand, opened a bag of chips, and began to reseal it with my new tool. The bag just ripped in half. The device did not seal anything! In fact, it did the opposite! "Okay," I said. "Maybe this is just a faulty bag. Let me try another one." I grabbed another bag of chips, and the same thing happened! The bag ripped in half! After two destroyed bags and the useless expenditure of six dollars and ninety-nine cents, I had a dull weight in the pit of my stomach telling me this idea might not work out.

Another product I ordered was a red portable soda dispenser. All you had to do was screw the soda bottle into the dispenser, and by pulling a tab, the soda would be poured right into a glass. It was more novel than practical, but I thought it was cool and would sell for sure. When it arrived, I decided to try it out, hoping it would not be a repeat of the sealer incident. When I screwed in a bottle of Coke, the bottle of Coke did not dispense. Instead, the bottle of Coke exploded and spilled all over the kitchen! Ugh! What a disaster.

Now to be fair, some of the products did end up working. For example, I ordered a pair of dishwashing gloves with tiny bristles, which made washing dishes fun! Okay, maybe not fun, but it made washing dishes easier. Despite this, most of the products that I sampled proved to cause more problems than they solved, so naturally, I had to rework my business plan. I went back to the drawing board (or, in my case, the computer), looking for new products with reliable manufacturers.

I finally settled on the name of the website: Unique Culinary Creations. After some brainstorming, I began designing the website so that it would be appealing to my customers. I created a compelling home page that would draw potential customers in. I also made a logo while I was in an artistic mood. After writing a mission statement, I wrote descriptions for each of my products; and even ran a banner across the top of the website that offered a 10 percent discount! I don't want to bore you with details, but you get the point—I improved the website and prepared to go to market.

In addition, I began learning about marketing strategies and how to promote the online store in the most economical way. I did not want to spend thousands of dollars on advertising fees, which forced me to learn how to market efficiently and stretch every dollar. I spoke with someone who had just launched his online business and learned from him. I asked him what worked and what he wished he had done differently. He was not selling kitchen gadgets, but some of the lessons and advice still applied to my venture. After this conversation, I altered my game plan slightly to maximize website visits, sales, and (hopefully) profits.

Having taken this path for a few months and learning the facets of an online business, I faced the fact that this idea wasn't going to pan out. So I reviewed the results.

Product Samples: -$150

Shopify Subscription: -$30

Domain: -$20

Sales: $0

Cost of Goods: $0

Net Gains: -$200

Yes, you read that right; I lost $200! What a failed venture, right? Not so fast! Financially, was it a failure? Sure. I mean, I did lose $200 in the process. But overall, I would actually argue that this business was a success and a worthwhile experience. And no, I'm not crazy! I know that losing $200 is not something to brag about.

You see, through this process, I was able to learn so much about business, sales, and entrepreneurship in general. I gained experience in creating and designing an aesthetically pleasing website that conveyed the brand's message and "tone." By creating Facebook advertisements for my website, I better understood the field of marketing and its importance. Moreover, I learned about deciding which products to sell by researching recent trends and the market's general direction. The opportunity to speak with manufacturers about price, delivery time, quality, and return policy allowed me to improve my business communication skills, which I am sure will help me down the road. I gained experience in pricing products not only to maximize profits but also to maintain as many customers as possible. I became more adept at writing/understanding legal documents, crafting compelling product descriptions, and making the check-out process as simple as possible. Even though I lost money through this venture, I gained so much knowledge that I don't regret it at all. Hands-on experience is just as necessary as textbook learning—and through this journey, I was able to partake in both methods of education.

I took action by starting this business. Even though it failed in the traditional definition, it succeeded in the sense that I learned from my mistakes and became a better business person. It would have been much more problematic if I had not learned these lessons, and some years later, I was dealing with $20,000, $100,000, or $1,000,000—and lost all of it.

*

TAKEAWAY

Thomas J. Watson, the founder of IBM, once said, "Would you like me to give you a formula for success? It's quite simple, really: Double your rate of failure. You are thinking of failure as the enemy of success. But it isn't at all. You can be discouraged by failure, or you can learn from it, so go ahead and make mistakes. Make all you can. Because remember that's where you will find success."

Psychologist Dr. Nigel Barber makes the point that failure teaches you to be more persistent and resilient, "Never underestimate the magical properties of failure. It rewires the brain and gets the creative juices flowing." I want to make something very clear: failure is only a learning opportunity if you actually learn from it. In his article entitled "6 Proven Strategies to Rebound from Failure," Deep Patel suggests asking the following questions:

- "What lessons did I learn from this situation?"

    - Sit down and think about what you now know that you did not know before. You have either learned a new skill or how to deal with a specific type of person. Either way, you learned something, and it is essential to recognize these lessons.

- "What are three positive outcomes of this situation?"

    - The experience may not have been great overall, but there had to be some positive aspects. Look on the bright side and be grateful for what went right and how it serves as a benefit for the future.

- "How has this experience allowed me to grow as a person?"

  - This is probably one of the most challenging questions, but it offers some valuable insight if you actually think about it. How have you changed from the experience? Consider your personality, skills, abilities to deal with certain situations, inner thoughts, relationships, confidence levels, and so on. Compare the person before the failed experience to the person you are today.

I want to leave you with one thought: Who would you rather be? Someone who has failed nine times and succeeded one time or someone who has failed zero times and succeeded zero times?

PART 2

HABITS

4

TRY NEW THINGS

―

"Life always begins with one step outside of your comfort zone."

—SHANNON L. ALDER

Would you consider yourself a picky eater? I'll admit it. I am a picky eater. When I find something I like, I will stick to it and eat it as often as possible. For example, I love pizza, and I would not mind eating it for lunch every day for a week. This being said, I have trouble trying new foods because there is no need to when I already have a few dishes that I really enjoy. I try my best to stay in my comfort zone so that I don't put myself in unfamiliar situations unnecessarily. In other words, trying new things—especially food—is challenging for me, and it is often easier to stick to what I know and love best: pizza.

Despite this, I have often found myself asking whether staying in my comfort zone is really the best course of action. The practice of trying new things allows you to become more creative, more adaptable, more resilient, and it offers numerous opportunities to learn something new. Although it is difficult to step out of your comfort zone, it is paramount for your professional success and personal growth.

*

CONSTRUCTION WITHOUT KNOWING CONSTRUCTION

"My whole life, we called [Delaware] the suburbs of Philadelphia jokingly because no one really knows where Delaware is," explained Brennan Stark. Brennan grew up in Northern Delaware and was the oldest of three children. He attended public school up to eighth grade and went to a private school after that. Even though he didn't realize it at the time, Brennan has been an entrepreneur since his youth. In elementary school, Brennan sold Silly Bandz to his classmates in exchange for pizza, chocolate milk, and sometimes cash. He has collected thousands of bands, and he and his friends expanded his Silly Band empire. In middle school, Brennan sold things on eBay as a virtual garage sale. In hindsight, he remarks, "I basically liquidated my entire room." As he matured, he collected sports memorabilia and sold them at higher prices.

When he started high school, Brennan did not feel satisfied with the content and material he was learning in school. He explained, "Something felt fundamentally unsatisfying about it. I felt like the things I was learning [wasn't applicable, and] I wasn't seeing how they were gonna actually have some sort of impact on the world." He wanted to do something more meaningful with his life rather than being an "ordinary" student.

One day, Brennan was hanging out with his friend, Steve. They were chatting about the importance of not being complacent with one's current situation and how instead, one should always look to improve. As conversations go, one thing turned to another, and the topic shifted toward housing. The friends began to discuss what the perfect house would entail. They brainstormed a bunch of ideas and sketched out different floorplans. The more time they spent talking and designing the perfect house, the more they came across these "natural builders," who constructed homes at an affordable cost. "They're just sort of hippies who lived off the grid, and they built houses really affordably. Like, $3,000 to build a new house."

They thought this was amazing but wondered how they could use this information to make the world better. Steve often volunteered at soup kitchens because there was a great deal of homeless people in Wilmington, Delaware. The two friends would often talk about the homeless population in conjunction with their passion for the "perfect house." And this was when the lightbulb went off. They launched Y Innovations, and their goal was to "build sustainable, affordable housing in inner-city Wilmington for low-income families."

And while this was a great idea, there was one problem—neither Brennan nor Steve knew anything about construction. Brennan encapsulated his thought process at the time as, "Oh shit, like we're saying we're going to do this, but how are we actually going to do it?" They felt they were not qualified to take on this endeavor and began to lose confidence. Brennan pointed out, "We didn't know about the permit process, we didn't know about how to raise money or start a nonprofit or anything like that."

He realized that they just needed to take one small step and use that momentum going forward. "I think the fundamental principle there was, we had to get over the fear, we had to do one thing, take one small step," explained Brennan.

Their first step was looking up how to build "cob houses" online. They found a PDF that outlined some of the instructions. They purchased some materials from Home Depot and played around in Brennan's backyard. Eventually, they came up with a recipe that yielded a somewhat usable brick. "The brick was not perfect, but it was fairly solid." They turned the brick into a wall unit and scaled that up into a house! They took one small step, which led to the next small step, which led to another—until they eventually got where they needed to be.

Brennan and his friend built a seven hundred square-foot home for a homeless father and son. The home is net-zero emissions because it is powered by solar panels. The family still lives in that home, and, in fact, they still keep in touch with Brennan. Because Brennan realized the importance of trying new things even if you feel lost, he was inspired to take concrete steps toward his dream. Not only was he able to achieve his goals—he was able to help a homeless family in need.

Brennan recognizes that many people fear failure and thus are not comfortable with taking that first step. However, instead of thinking about the risk of embarking on a new journey, think about the risk of inaction and consider the opportunity cost if you don't try something new. Opportunity costs and the experiences you missed out on may not seem significant right now; however, as time progresses, these missed opportunities compound, and the effects become apparent when considering what your life could have been. In other words, "Nothing is more expensive than a missed opportunity."

Fast-forward five, ten, twenty, or even fifty years: Would you rather have tried something new, failed, taken those lessons, and applied them to your next venture, or not done it at all and wonder what could have been? And who knows, maybe that one attempt won't be a failure; perhaps it will be a massive success. But you will never find out until you give it a shot!

Today, Brennan is a graduate of the University of Delaware. He is currently working on Peerpal, an educational tech company working with over two hundred schools. He is excited to change industries and try new things because even if it scares him and even if he feels like an imposter, he knows there is a myriad of benefits.

According to an article from the *Huffington Post* entitled "6 Reasons to Step Outside Your Comfort Zone," trying new things and stretching your comfort zone helps with creativity (Gregoire, 2014). In fact, research shows that students who challenged themselves and studied abroad reported higher levels of creativity compared to their counterparts. But is this really a surprise? When we explore new passions, interests, and aspects of the world, we are introduced to so much more than we ever imagined existed. This exposure allows us to not only better understand the world around us but also the person inside of us. Creativity is not a science, but science shows that trying new things contributes significantly to our creative abilities.

I want you to consider a scenario where you live in a small town. This could be one hundred people, one thousand people, or five thousand people—however you imagine a small town. No one is allowed to leave this town, and so, you never do. You get used to the people around you as you see them walking their dog past your house, you get to know the local barista at the coffee shop, and you say "Hi" to the mailman every day. Activities are limited in the town, and the only thing you can really do is go for a walk around the neighborhood. In other words, you are smack-dab in the center of your comfort zone, and nothing new ever happens. In this scenario, I want you to rate how creative you think you'd be on a scale from one to ten.

Now, imagine that the town's rules have changed, and you are promptly permitted to enter and leave as you please. You bravely decide to explore the area around your town, meet new people, engage in new activities, and try new things. Maybe you take up painting or learn how to ride a bike. Perhaps you start a band or travel the world. Whatever it may be, it might be terrifying because you are used to living in a protected bubble where nothing ever changed. However, you are now exploring new aspects of the world and are unsure what will happen next. At this point in the scenario, I want you to rate your creativity on a scale from one to ten. Do you think it would be higher than your previous rating?

It's not easy stepping out of your comfort zone and putting yourself in uncomfortable situations. However, doing so allows you to explore things you had not considered before, thus opening your eyes to the world around you and boosting your creativity. This new creativity can be beneficial in a multitude of ways, from starting a business and being a leader to making a new friend and striking up a conversation with them. Creativity has its benefits, and creativity is fostered by uncomfortable situations and stretching your comfort zone.

Trying new things and scaring yourself allows you to learn and gain experience, as can be evidenced by the story of Ed Helms. You are probably wondering what Ed Helms—an actor and comedian—is doing in a book about business and entrepreneurship. The truth is, his advice to explore new aspects of life applies to everyone, especially entrepreneurs and changemakers.

*

ED HELMS AND HIS FOOLISHNESS

During his commencement speech at Cornell University, Ed Helms shared a fundamental lesson he had garnered from personal experience. The lesson in question? *Be a fool.* This sounds crazy, but Ed discovered the importance of this after playing Andy Bernard in NBC's show *The Office*. "Andy, by all accounts, was a fool—a glorious, vulnerable fool," explained Ed. He wanted to be more like Andy because of his foolish nature and willingness to try new things, despite his fear. Ed stated, "Foolishness is a condescending word for joy, wonder, and curiosity" and "the world provides us with virtually infinite opportunities to be a fool." Reflecting back on his earlier years, Ed pointed out the importance of being a fool and trying new things, even when you are unsure what the outcome will be.

Ed went to college with a man named Phil Manley, who would later go on to form part of the band Trans Am. After graduation, Phil and his music buddies became successful indie rock stars, while Ed moved to New York City to be a filmmaker and comedian. Ed called Phil one day and asked, "Hey Phil, can I direct a music video for you guys?" Naturally, Phil replied, "I don't know. What are your qualifications?" Ed responded, "I don't have any." Somehow, Phil agreed to let Ed take control of their next music video.

At the time, Ed was living with some college friends in Brooklyn, and as soon as Ed got the gig to direct the music video, he reached out to his friends and all of their friends so they could host a full-blown Trans Am concert. They did just this in a warehouse and planned to record the music video during the performance. Ed was very nervous because he was wearing multiple hats. He was the concert promoter, the cameraman, the video director, the hair and makeup artist, and the set designer. To make matters worse, Ed had no idea what he was doing.

The video production was a complete failure. The film in the camera jammed, Ed could not control the people during a rock concert, drunk people threw props into the river, and Ed lost his temper. "The video was awful," described Ed. "I was a fool for taking on more than I could handle [...] but at least I had an outcome, and outcomes, whether good or bad, allow us to move forward." Had he not been a fool and tried something new, he would have never had this learning experience. Rather, he would have a sense of regret "which is at best useless and at worse, paralyzing."

After his music video directing career went down the drain, Ed landed a stable job. And as if he hadn't been foolish enough, he quit this job to make a full-time career out of comedy. "Only a fool would work hard when there is no clear objective. Be that fool," said Ed. He did not know where his comedy career was going to take him, but he was willing to try something new and work hard to reach his dreams.

It would be a long time before Ed made money from comedy. To support himself, he recorded commercial voiceovers for the radio. He went to hundreds of auditions all over Manhattan and booked 1 percent of them, at best. The other 99 percent "went up in smoke," as Ed pointed out. While these seemed like wastes of time and foolish decisions, Ed continued auditioning, which built up his confidence. He did not experience the show-business nerves anymore. He would, in his words, "walk in, do his thing, and walk out." This was very beneficial because when Ed auditioned for a part that he really wanted on *The Daily Show*, he walked into the audition calm, cool, and collected. And guess what? He got the part!

Later on, Ed was invited to play the role of Andy Bernard on *The Office*; however, there was one problem. The character was only supposed to be on the show for eight episodes (amounting to eight weeks). "Could I really quit my job at *The Daily Show* for only eight weeks of work?" Should he really be a fool and try something new? As you probably have guessed by now, he did. "I foolishly took the role of Andy Bernard," said Ed. "After six episodes, I became a permanent cast member, and I was employed for not only eight weeks, but eight wonderful years."

This was not (nor will it ever be) the last time Ed experienced a decision to try something new. When he got the script for

The Hangover, he was not sure if he wanted to take the role. Would it ruin his reputation as an actor and comedian? He decided to accept the part, and it was a great experience. As an actor, singer, and comedian who has appeared in dozens of films and television shows, Ed has had a great deal of experience. Through it all, however, he has learned the importance of being a fool and trying new things!

Being a fool and putting yourself in uncomfortable situations allows you to learn and grow. In fact, "doing hard things 70 percent of the time" is the best way to maximize your learning, according to Auren Hoffman, a five-time entrepreneur (Stillman 2018). Furthermore, Brené Brown, a research professor at the University of Houston, explained that one of the worst things we can do is pretend fear and uncertainty don't exist (Henry, Fishbein 2019). "By taking risks in a controlled fashion and challenging yourself to things you normally wouldn't do, you can experience some of that uncertainty in a controlled, manageable environment." This allows you to learn how to deal with uncomfortable situations when you are thrown into them without having a choice. Think about it as swimming in the ocean. Say that you hate swimming because you have a fear of drowning. Wouldn't it be better to practice swimming in a controlled, safe environment so that if you do get thrown into the water, you can survive? Being in uncomfortable situations is no different. Practice allows you to learn how to cope with these situations if they are thrown at you at the worst times.

While describing their recent study, Daeyeol Lee—a neuroscientist at Yale University—stated, "perhaps the most important insight from our study is that the function of the brain, as well as the nature of learning, is not 'fixed' but adapts according to the stability of the environment [...] When you enter a more novel and volatile environment, this might enhance the tendency for the brain to absorb more information." It has become evident that uncomfortable situations and the practice of stretching our comfort zones allow us to learn more, which has many benefits.

In addition, trying new things is sometimes the push we need to take on our next venture and embark on the next journey. But, why take it from me when you can learn about it through the experiences of Gabrielle Jordan?

*

JEWELZ OF JORDAN
At the age of seven, Gabrielle Jordan was in love with jewelry. She would spend hours a day watching YouTube videos about jewelry and reading magazines to find design ideas. She even made her own jewelry at home using her creativity. When she wore her pieces to school, her classmates fell in love with them. In her TEDx Talk, Gabrielle explains, "My friends would buy them right off of me."

She had a dream to start her own jewelry business but feared that no one would buy her pieces. She could be wasting time, people could make fun of her, and/or the company could miserably fail. Recognizing that fear was holding her daughter back from achieving her true potential, Gabrielle's mother gave her a book by Spencer Johnson titled *Who Moved My Cheese?* This book had a powerful quote that resonated with Gabrielle: "What would you do if you weren't afraid?" This future entrepreneur wrote this quote down on a piece of paper, taped it to her bedroom wall, and looked at it every day. This way, she could acknowledge her fear but be able to overcome it at the same time. At the age of nine, Gabrielle started Jewelz of Jordan, the business she dreamed of running. Through her website as well as retailers, she sold her jewelry to all types of people. She wasn't sure how this venture would turn out, but she wanted to try something new: running a business at a young age.

When Gabrielle walked into her first trade show, she immediately noticed that all of the vendors were adults who were selling jewelry featured in famous magazines. After that sight, Gabrielle assumed she wasn't going to sell anything. The host of the trade show passed around a microphone so all the vendors could introduce themselves. This was difficult for Gabrielle because she was already so nervous and felt like a fish out of water. When the microphone came to her, she stuttered, got out a few incoherent words, and passed the microphone to the next person. However, this is how Gabrielle describes her performance, purely from her point of view. One's personal perception can vastly differ from what others see, and this situation was no exception.

People came up to Gabrielle during the trade show saying, "Oh, you did great." "Are they crazy?" thought Gabrielle, "I did horrible." Again, she did horrible in her eyes. People were genuinely impressed with her business, and they were inspired to see someone chase after their dreams at such a young age. At the event, Gabrielle ended up selling out of almost everything. This inspired her to go home, try new things with her business, and continue following her dreams.

At the age of eleven, Gabrielle wrote a book about her entrepreneurial experiences entitled *The Making of a Young Entrepreneur: A Kid's Guide to Developing the Mindset For Success*. She even gives a portion of the book profits to organizations that help those in need. She is currently the cofounder of ExCel Youth Mentoring Institute, a youth-based online mentoring organization. She is also a TEDx speaker, the host of the UV Effect Products, and has been featured in publications such as TLC, *Huffington Post*, and the *Harry* show. Gabrielle's mentality to try something new has led to so many amazing things. Had she never embarked on this journey and attempted something she was uncomfortable with, she would not have the same impact that she does today.

Gabrielle's mentality to try new things has likely been a critical component of both her company's success and her own personal victories. According to the Bureau of Labor Statistics, 20 percent of businesses fail within their first two years (Deane 2020). Forty-five percent fail during their first five years and 65 percent in their first ten years. In fact, only 25 percent of businesses make it to fifteen years of age. Now, I don't give you these numbers to make you upset or discouraged; instead, I am telling you this to raise the question: "Why do so many start-ups fail?" To be honest, there is no straightforward answer to this question. Michael T. Deane explained in an Investopedia article that "being too rigid" is one of the top six reasons why companies fail (Deane 2020). In other words, their failure to adapt and try new approaches is what leads to their demise. At the end of the day, entrepreneurship is about trying things, failing, and then trying again. If we are too rigid and refuse to stretch our comfort zone, how can we expect to succeed? This mentality not only applies to companies but to individuals as well. If we as individuals are too rigid and are opposed to trying new things, we will never reach our true potential. Remember, Gabrielle would have never started her jewelry business if it wasn't for her desire to try something new.

*

TAKEAWAY

In an article for the *Huffington Post*, Leon Logothetis explains that one way to force yourself out of your comfort zone is to take small, baby steps (Logothetis 2018). This is much easier than throwing yourself into a situation that you fear, and over time these baby steps will add up, and you will have the courage to really explore the world around you. An article from the *Huffington Post* also advises to "make snap decisions, and make a fool of yourself." Does that sound familiar to Ed Helms? Stop overthinking every little decision you make and embrace the idea of spontaneity. Lastly, do something that scares you every day. For some, this may be talking to a stranger. For others, it could be asking your crush out on a date. Your "scary" actions do not need to be related to business; rather, they should aim to instill the "try something new" mentality in your head.

I am not going to sit here and act like stepping out of your comfort zone is easy—because it's not. However, your abilities and success are just like muscles. They need to be stretched and exercised in different ways if you want them to grow. So do your best to try new things because you will never experience life outside of your bubble unless you actually leave it.

5

POWER OF PURPOSE

"No one can capitalize on this economy better than someone who is driven to make a difference in people's lives."
—WENDY LIPTON-DIBNER

Private jets, yachts, luxury vacations, exotic cars, and mansions—these are some of the reasons why most people want to be an entrepreneur. People hope to make millions, if not billions, of dollars off of their business. After all, isn't the whole point of business about making money?

While making money is a significant component of being an entrepreneur, it should not be the main priority. When you focus on the purpose of the business and what impact it has on the community, you will yield maximum success. This can be seen through Siddarth Sridhar's story of when he was in high school.

*

HELPING THE ENVIRONMENT WHILE HELPING OTHERS

As cliché as it might sound, when Siddarth Sridhar was a young child in New Jersey, he decided to start a lemonade stand. He was younger than the other children in his neighborhood, so, naturally, he felt a little intimidated. Despite this, he embarked on his journey to sell lemonade to the masses. Siddarth set up his stand in high traffic areas so he could get more customers. I wish I had thought of that when I was a kid! This genius tactic paid off. He sold a great deal of lemonade, and as a result, he made a lot of money.

The problem was, however, that Siddarth did not know what to do with the profits. He was a young child being supported by his parents, and Siddarth recognized that other people needed the money more than he did.

In fact, Siddarth has a cousin who is autistic; and growing up with them allowed Siddarth to see what his cousin's life was like. Because of his personal connection to the cause, Siddarth thought it would be most appropriate to donate his lemonade proceeds to an autism charity. This was nothing more than a kind-hearted gesture on Siddarth's end. Though, what no one knew was that he would continue to make a profound impact on his community in the future.

Fast-forward six years to when Siddarth was starting high school. Initially, he wanted to be a doctor because he really enjoyed his biology class and his mother was in the field of medicine. However, he eventually realized that going to medical school was not something he was genuinely interested in. His second thought initially was to become an investment banker instead. Still, he always left his options open by exploring his other passions and interests.

A cardinal turning point in Siddarth's life occurred when he spent a week at his father's workplace. His father worked in consulting, and thus, Siddarth was given the opportunity to learn different business skills and understand how companies operate. This intrigued him, and he later started TILE (Talks on Innovation, Leadership, and Entrepreneurship) at his school. The goal was to bring in guest speakers to talk to high school students about developing the soft skills they needed in business and everyday life. Siddarth brought in speakers such as the person who ran his local newspaper and a financial commentator from *The New York Times*.

After hearing from numerous speakers, the ambitious teenager wanted to follow their lead and help those around him. Don't get me wrong, Siddarth loved hearing from experts, but he also wanted to put those skills into play and support his community.

During my interview with Siddarth, he recalled an experience that he had almost five years ago. In eighth grade, his grandmother passed away, and he and his family went to a village in India to spread her ashes. India has a lot of pollution and smog. Siddarth recognized these environmental issues as soon as he got off of the plane. He and his family traveled to the village and began to eat a meal.

At that moment, Siddarth noticed something interesting: the villagers were serving food on plates made out of leaves. They were trying to be sustainable and efficient to help the environment. These plates were microwave safe, made using a steam-press technology, and "you can throw it in your backyard, and it's going to biodegrade in a week." As a result, these plates were helping the environment since they were reducing the amount of plastic being used. "I was intrigued by this," explained Siddarth. "This did great for India, so why not for Uncle Sam?" In other words, he wanted to bring this innovative way of serving food to the United States.

Later on, Siddarth began speaking with his parents about the experience he had in India and how he wanted to introduce eco-friendly plates to the United States. He talked to his parents, and together they decided on how to make this business a reality. "I conceived this, I made a plan, and they were like, 'Let's do this!'" said Siddarth. He launched VerDay Inc. and started selling plates in New Jersey. But he soon began to get orders from Texas, California, and other states that he did not directly sell to. He and his team would source materials, sell them, and invest the profits into developing new products. For example, he came out with a line of oven-safe and freezer-safe cups, and those were a huge hit!

At this point, Siddarth had made a large sum of money; however, he then faced a considerable dilemma. "I am a seventeen-year-old. What do I do with the money?" Siddarth asked himself. His family was financially stable, and he thought it would be selfish to keep the money for himself. Does this story sound familiar? Yes, it does! It is the same situation he faced with his lemonade stand almost eight years ago. And yes, the solution was the same. Siddarth pondered, "Well, why don't I start donating this money toward charitable causes for autistic youth in my community?"

And he did just that. This generous and creative teenager explained, "People don't start companies to become rich, and if you do, you probably shouldn't start a company." To him, the perk of his venture was helping the community and society as a whole.

This young entrepreneur would go to different trade shows in his Indian community to advertise and sell his product. "I was very tired one day," said Siddarth, and he began to think to himself, "Why am I doing this? What's the point?" He was traveling every weekend for his business, he was constantly tired, and he wanted to give up.

"That's when a nice, Indian lady [came] up to our booth." She asked Siddarth a question that he describes as "the most sincere question I have ever heard someone ask." This young woman asked him, "Do they have programs at your high school for autistic youth?" The woman then pointed to her son, who could not have been older than three years old. "My son is autistic. I get worried for him sometimes because I feel that when he grows up, he might not have the opportunity to experience life as others would." I cannot imagine what that must feel like, and at that moment, Siddarth understood what he was fighting for. "I wanted to kick myself," said Siddarth. "Man, I'm an asshole for thinking the way I was thinking two minutes before."

"This moment always sticks in my mind because this is the moment that I figured out I am not going to stop this [his effort to help autistic youth]." Seeing the impact that you are having on society "should always be your fishing line back to reality" and convince you to keep working and pushing forward.

After this life-altering moment at the trade show, Siddarth truly understood the importance of helping others and not being selfish. Focusing on the impact and how you are making a difference in the world is what drives success.

Siddarth is currently a student at the University of California, Berkeley. But he hopes to combine his love of entrepreneurship, technology, and sustainability in the future. He is also a big fan of cleantech and hopes to get involved in this space someday. In addition, Siddarth would like to immerse himself in the world of venture capital and fund management. Overall, he is looking to make the world a better place through his selfless acts!

Believe it or not, a whopping 66 percent of consumers said they would be willing to switch who they buy a particular product from to support a purpose-driven company. This statistic takes all demographics into account—but when focusing just on millennials, this number jumps to 91 percent (Aziz 2020). Don't believe me? Imagine yourself in a scenario where you had a choice to purchase from either a money-hungry company or a business that aims to support abandoned puppies by encouraging people to donate. Which would you choose?

In addition, two out of every three consumers are willing to pay a price premium if that company makes a positive impact on the world (Aziz 2020). If that wasn't enough, consider the statistics that Wendy Lipton-Dibner—author and entrepreneur—uncovered when consulting for a telecom company (Conner 2015). The company was willing to shift its focus away from money and toward success, as Lipton-Dinner suggested. She brought the executives through a three-day training program, and the results were out of this world. Each sales team increased its revenue by at least 200 percent. And no, I did not add an extra zero by mistake.

The more money a company earns, the more of an impact it can make, which is exactly what Siddarth did in his venture. This philosophy and insight have made companies massive fortunes. Take Bombas as an example. They started selling socks and eventually moved to T-shirts, and for every article of clothing sold, they donate an article to a homeless shelter. Within five years of launching the business, Bombas had over $100 million in revenue and donated over ten million pairs of socks in just one year.

Not only does having a purpose at the center of the venture yield more money and help others, but it also creates momentum, thus benefiting society even more. Suppose you have a purpose that you are deeply passionate about at the core of your business. In that case, you are more likely to spend more time with this venture, work harder, and eventually watch it impact others. For example, if you are passionate about climate change and then start an organization (either for-profit or nonprofit) that helps to combat the deadly effects of the climate crisis, you are going to care more about this project and put more time into it, thus allowing it to have an actual impact. This was no different for Satvik Sethi.

*

MENTAL HEALTH ADVOCACY

In New Delhi, India, Satvik Sethi grew up in a household that always emphasized the virtues of giving and helping others. He and his family would donate money to those who needed it, feed underprivileged kids, and volunteer at different organizations. Satvik pointed out that because these values were instilled in him at such a young age, it made him a more empathetic person.

When Satvik began middle school, he and many of his friends were struggling with mental health problems. He dealt with bullying and exclusion while he had friends with eating disorders and self-harming habits. Satvik explained that, at a young age, "You don't really know that these are mental health problems. To you, these are just issues that you're having. [It] seem[s] like you're not gonna get out or you don't know how to deal with them." This was especially difficult for Satvik and his friends because the discussion of mental illness is often stigmatized in India. Satvik had his parents to talk to when he was going through a hard time, but unfortunately, a lot of his friends did not have people to talk to or people they could go to for support. "So for them, hiding their emotional distress was their way of dealing with it," explained Satvik. Because of his empathetic nature, people at school started to talk to Satvik about what they were going through. He was the person at school who anybody could go to and vent, ask for advice, or just talk to if they needed to. Satvik was there for everyone. "That was kind of my start into the whole mental health journey without even knowing that this is a mental health journey," said Satvik.

About one year later, Satvik was simply looking at Instagram, and he came across an image of someone self-harming (at the time, Instagram did not have any sort of censorship measures implemented, so people could post whatever they wanted to). He commented on the post and wrote, "If you need a friend to talk to, I'm there." Little did Satvik know that those ten words would change someone's life. This person actually reached out to him. They had a conversation, and Satvik was able to support them and help them cope with what was happening in their lives.

He found the act of helping others to be a very fulfilling experience, and he wanted to help more people. Satvik would spend time every day talking to people and helping them through their situations. In fact, over the next few years (before he even graduated high school), he had spoken to over 450 people. When he told his family about what he was doing, their first response was, "Why are you talking to people with mental illness?" They advised him to stop talking to these people and spend his time elsewhere. "At that moment, I had to make a decision whether to keep doing this or to stop because my parents told me to." Luckily, Satvik continued to help these people, but he had to do so in secrecy due to his parents' disapproval.

Shortly after, Satvik graduated high school and went to the US for college. Being an international student, Satvik was going through mental health problems of his own. Considering Satvik's emphatic nature, he obviously wanted to keep helping people via Instagram, but because his mental health was suffering, he found it challenging to be there for others.

Satvik came up with an app idea (which would eventually come to fruition as "Runway App"). This platform would allow people to talk anonymously to volunteers about their mental health problems. The only challenge with creating this app was the fact that Satvik "had zero technical expertise." His goal was to build an app, but he had no tech team. However, Satvik was dedicated to making an impact, and he was not going to stop at the first roadblock he encountered. He made a website on Wix and reached out to friends and family to see if they would help him. Some of his peers agreed to support him, but even after gaining some traction, Satvik still did not have an app.

Not wanting to halt the progress he was already making, Satvik hosted a mental health event on his college campus, and over two hundred people showed up. Satvik talked about what he learned from all the Instagram conversations. The overall goal of this event was to raise awareness and support those who needed it. Shortly after this event, Mental Health America reached out to him and invited him to join its Youth Mental Health Innovation Council. Later, he was offered speaking engagements—and even spoke at the United Nations.

His opportunities began to snowball, and, as a result, Satvik was given more and more chances to spread information about mental health awareness. This led to publicity and recognition around the Runaway App and Satvik's organization. More people began to volunteer, and today his team consists of over one hundred student volunteers around the world. In addition, Runaway App now has over one thousand beta testers for the app, and they are expecting massive progress. Satvik made an interesting point during our interview when he said, "I never started [Runaway App] to make money." Instead, he did it because he wanted to help others. "I think that's the power of purpose," said Satvik. "I think now a lot of young entrepreneurs want to do things because it looks good on a résumé [and it] makes them money. You might reap the rewards in the short-term, but you're not going to be passionate and consistent about it in the long-term." One of the first people Satvik ever messaged recently reached out to him and said, "I just graduated college and got my dream job as a photographer. If it wasn't for you that one night, I might not be here." These are the experiences that validate what Satvik is doing. And in case you were wondering, Satvik's family now fully supports what he is doing, and they are proud of him.

In the future, Satvik wants to make Runaway App accessible to everyone and be a part of mental health research. He also wants to continue advocating more mental health awareness and ensuring that needed resources are available to everyone. All in all, he wants to make the world a happier place!

Satvik makes an essential point that passion and purpose are critical in the long run. Studies have shown that purpose-driven companies grow at a much higher rate compared to their counterparts. Over twelve years, it has been found that companies with a low positive impact grew 70 percent, companies with a medium positive impact grew 86 percent, and companies with high positive impact grew 175 percent (Aziz 2020). Having an authentic purpose that you are passionate about provides you with the motivation you need to grow your venture and reach the success it deserves. If you think this lesson only applies to Satvik, think again because Alexa Kayman had a similar experience when it came to impact.

*

AN OPPORTUNITY TO PROVIDE OPPORTUNITIES

Alexa Kayman grew up in New York City. She describes herself as a fortunate child who was raised by a well-off family. However, from an early age, Alexa understood that not everyone in her community—or the world—was as fortunate as her in terms of living conditions, resources, and opportunities. This idea always stayed with her.

As a young child, Alexa enjoyed school; however, she got bored easily since she wanted to do more with her time to explore her passions and interests. As an enthusiastic, unique, and nonconforming student, Alexa thought entrepreneurship might be the thing for her. She started a business in fourth grade and tried to sell shoes with springs on them so people could jump higher. I know my fourth-grade self would've died for a pair of these shoes. Gym basketball, look out! In all seriousness, even though Alexa's business did not have a billion-dollar IPO (Initial Public Offering), she learned a great deal about starting a company—foreshadowing her future endeavors.

After realizing how lucky she was to grow up in a well-off family, Alexa wanted to start a mentorship program that connected underserved students to unique opportunities and various career fields. She launched the Generation, which "is [an online] social enterprise connecting underserved students to dedicated mentors, courses, opportunities, and learning resources for the careers of the future." The Generation continued to expand, and more students joined the platform. Since the courses they wanted to offer were not ready yet, Alexa and the Generation started offering internships to underprivileged kids looking for experience in specific fields—through what they called the "Opportunity Center."

Some students signed up for this service, but Alexa and her team realized that the people signing up were not their intended demographic. Instead, they were "students from elite public schools and mostly New York City private schools that already had access to these resources." Alexa realized she was straying away from her mission and purpose, and thus she had to change something. She realized privileged students were signing up for opportunities because they already knew what they were interested in. On the other hand, many underprivileged kids did not know what they wanted to explore, and thus they did not sign up. For example, someone who had many resources as a child might already recognize that they want to pursue finance, so they sign up for a finance internship. However, someone who lacked certain resources as a child might not even realize they have a passion for finance. After Alexa understood what the problem was, she changed the "Opportunity Center" to the "Resource Center," where students could explore their passions and figure out what they enjoyed by trying different activities. This way, the efforts of Alexa and her team were going toward people who actually needed it.

At this point, the Generation had gained some traction, but it was not doing exceptionally well. Alexa explained, "There were regular signups every now and then, but it didn't really feel like I was making an impact. Sometimes I even felt that I needed to lie to myself when I looked at the metrics on our platform." As a result, Alexa began to question if what she was doing was even worth it. If this platform was not going to have an impact, why was she spending so much time on it? This is a thought many entrepreneurs face, and Alexa is no exception. She felt like quitting. That was when she heard about a young girl from

Southern Texas who was using the Generation. This girl, who could not afford many opportunities as a child, reached out to Alexa to say that the Generation connected her with a $45,000 "Women in STEM" scholarship for college. This changed this young girl's life, and it allowed her to attend her dream college. After hearing from this girl, and many other stories from people in similar situations, Alexa knew it would be selfish to shut down the Generation because she indeed was having an impact. "It's sort of a reminder that there are people depending on this platform, and that definitely gives me a mission and drive to continue doing it," said Alexa.

Currently, the Generation is helping and supporting over ten thousand students, and Alexa reached out to students to learn more about them and form a deeper relationship. While Alexa is most definitely interested in expanding the Generation, she is more interested in helping students. She pointed out, "Even though, as a tech platform, there are a lot of other ways that we could be more profitable, and maybe expand faster, but that's just not what we're looking for in our mission." Her wholehearted purpose, along with her mission and the inspiring stories she hears, reminds her of the impact she has on the world.

Looking to the future, Alexa wants to continue working on the Generation and making learning resources accessible. In fact, they have not even come out with their main courses yet, so they are excited to see what impact that has. Alexa continues to explore entrepreneurship, marketing, digital strategies, and even politics. But overall, her experiences from the Generation will always remind her of the importance of having a purpose and understanding how you are helping others.

Seventy-three percent of consumers said they would be willing to defend a purpose-driven company if it is attacked and its reputation begins to tarnish (Aziz 2020). Alexa's mission and purpose make people appreciate what she is doing, which not only helps her but also helps her organization help others.

*

TAKEAWAY

Money is obviously a prominent aspect of life, but that does not mean purpose should be devalued in any way. In fact, having a purpose often leads to a clearer path and thus results in more success (including financially). When you work on something you are genuinely passionate about, you will enjoy spending time with the project and be more likely to go the extra mile.

Having a solid foundation and reason for what you are doing will serve as a constant reminder to keep pushing forward even when times get tough. Why are you doing this, and why do you really care about this purpose?

Simon Sinek put it best when he said, "When we help ourselves, we find moments of happiness. When we help others, we find lasting fulfillment."

6

ALWAYS LEARN

"Give a man a fish and you feed him for a day. Teach him how to fish and you feed him for a lifetime"
—LAO TZU (CHINESE PHILOSOPHER)

Throughout your life, you can probably recall *those* moments at the dinner table where your parents would ask the famous line, "So what did you learn today in school?" It's safe to assume that most teenagers worldwide would usually respond with the same answer: "Nothing." I mean, why would you want to talk about education and the school day after school is over?

Is learning really that important? Many people think once you become an adult, you won't need to learn anymore. While this may be true to an extent, the notion of learning does not *completely* go away after high school or college. Sure, your future education may not be traditional in the sense that you are sitting in a classroom listening to a teacher explain how to find the volume of a sphere. However, be it through conversations, books, media, or other types of content, learning every day is a valuable activity to engage in.

No matter where you are in your life, having the mentality and itinerary of a lifelong learner (such as reading books and having intellectual conversations) is beneficial in more ways than can be imagined. This concept can and will help you not only professionally and financially but also personally and socially. Whether you are a four-year-old child learning to ride your bike for the first time or an eighty-year-old grandparent trying to keep up with the latest technological advancements—learning is a critical aspect of life that must be embraced.

*

THE IMPACT OF AN EARLY LESSON
Mark Cuban was born in 1958 to a middle-class family in Pittsburg, Pennsylvania. His father worked in an upholstery shop, while his mother worked various odd-jobs. Neither of his parents attended college, and therefore, he did not have as many resources as his peers did. Ever since Mark was a child, he was interested in business and entrepreneurship; more specifically, he was eager to learn more about these fields academically. He would read business books while his friends went to the movies, and he would read newspapers reporting on business news while his peers were out on the playground. He was a tenacious and persistent child who would go far in life.

One day, Mark wanted to get a new pair of shoes that he could play basketball in and wear to school. While his father was playing a game of poker with his friends, Mark went up to him and asked if he would buy him the new high tops. His father simply replied, "Those shoes on your feet look like they're working pretty well. If you want a new pair of sneakers, you need a job, and you can go buy them." This was a wrench in twelve-year-old Mark Cuban's plan to get a brand-new pair of sneakers, something he had wanted for a long time. As persistent as Mark was, he tried and tried again to get his father to pay for the shoes, but time and time again, his father explained that if Mark wanted new shoes, Mark would have to pay for them.

Like any twelve-year-old child who has been told "No," Mark was not happy; rather, he was frustrated. He responded to his father by saying, "Dad, I'm twelve years old; where am I gonna get a job?" That's when one of his father's buddies stepped in and explained he had some garbage bags he needed to sell, and Mark could go door-to-door selling them. The box of one hundred garbage bags would cost Mark three dollars, and he would sell them for six dollars, leaving him a three-dollar profit per unit. While this may not seem like a lot, Mark only needed to sell enough bags to finance his brand-new shoes, and he took the first opportunity he got to get there.

So, Mark set off and made it his goal to become a garbage bag salesman in his neighborhood. He would go door-to-door and say, "Hi, does your family use garbage bags?" Obviously, almost everyone said, "Yes." This question would be Mark's key to success in that job. It made the customer admit they had a need for Mark's product, and thus half of his selling process was already completed. Mark would then conveniently put forward his offer and explain why it's a good deal for them. Plus, who could turn away a twelve-year-old kid walking door-to-door selling garbage bags?

Eventually, Mark was able to sell enough bags to buy his new pair of shoes, but that was not nearly the most important outcome of this endeavor. He had gained the confidence and experience to sell products and ultimately be an entrepreneur at such a young age. Mark put in the time to learn about business not only through books and newspapers but also through experiences such as selling garbage bags to his neighbors. In a video entitled "Mark Cuban Gives Advice to Teen Entrepreneurs," Mark explained he "found success because I [Mark] was willing to put in the time." Impressed with the positive outcome of the garbage bag journey, he began collecting stamps and coins and selling them to others because he believes "what works once can work twice."

And while he was definitely a successful teen entrepreneur, his endeavors extended far beyond his childhood. During college, he was always involved in entrepreneurial ventures that included providing dance lessons and even opening a bar on campus. After graduating, many of his classmates were happy to find full-time jobs, but Mark knew he wanted to do more with his life. He started and sold multiple companies, and he has made large sums of money from them. Today, Mark is the billionaire owner of the Dallas Mavericks and a star on the hit television series *Shark Tank*.

Despite his massive success, Mark emphasizes the importance of constantly learning. Even now, he is always reading about new technology and how it will change the world. Don't be surprised if you find him in one of your online classes because he is constantly taking introductory courses in different subjects to expand his knowledge, which will ultimately assist his multiple businesses.

Whether it be to his kids, family members, friends, colleagues, or young entrepreneurs, Mark is always encouraging education and learning because "the one thing in life you can control is your effort."

In Cathy Davidson's 2012 book, *Now You See It: How Technology and Brain Science Will Transform Schools and Business for the 21st Century,* she writes, "65 percent of children entering grade school this year [2012] will end up working in careers that haven't even been invented yet." If that isn't shocking enough to see how the world is adjusting, consider how a 2014 report showed that 50 percent of jobs would be redundant by 2025 due to advancing technology (Newman 2017). It would be quite a tall order to try to stop the world from evolving. So, the only way to keep up with this movement is to advance ourselves. How can we do that? We can do that by learning! It does not just need to be on a technological basis; lifelong learning allows us to keep up with the current state of society from a plethora of standpoints.

Not only this, but it also often yields immense benefits in terms of your career. Research has shown that of the adults who have taken a class in the past year, 65 percent said it expanded their professional network, 47 percent indicated it helped them advance in their current company, 29 percent found a new job due to their class, and 27 percent said it encouraged them to think about a different career path (Winerman 2017). The numbers don't add up to 100 percent because participants were allowed to list more than one benefit. Nevertheless, the evidence is clear: with the changing times, learning is paramount no matter what impact you hope to make or what business you dream of starting. But don't think that knowledge only yields financial results. It produces personal developments, too. Take it from Malekai Mischke.

*

EXPERIENCE: THE FOUNDATION OF LEARNING

Malekai Mischke grew up and spent the vast majority of his childhood in Beijing, China, since he was half Chinese. He went to an international school filled with students from around the world. His classmates were all unique, and their parents were different from the norm, too, due to their uncommon and often exciting jobs. Malekai explained this environment "made [him] want to be unique and interesting at all times." One way Malekai began to become a unique individual was when he started to play sports and devote a large portion of his day to becoming a better athlete. "To be honest, all I cared about growing up was sports," Malekai pointed out.

After graduating high school, Malekai went to college in the United States and played basketball as a student-athlete. As a college student, he also went on to intern for several corporate organizations. But, as it turns out, he did not enjoy that experience at all. He wanted to do something different, more fulfilling with his life.

Upon college graduation, Malekai and two of his friends started a digital coupon company called Recoup, which would distribute online coupons of local businesses to nearby students, increasing traffic for the business and offering discounts to students. Because both he and the people he started the company with were international students, they needed "real" jobs to secure their visas. Unfortunately, for this reason, the company fell apart. Malekai elaborated, "We didn't make it work long-term, but I learned a lot in the process, and I learned most importantly that I'm passionate about this entrepreneurship game."

In the fall of 2018—shortly after graduating college and the demise of Recoup—Malekai decided he wanted to teach English to students in Italy. While the experience was worthwhile because he got to meet different people, travel, and teach English to those who didn't speak it, Malekai did not feel fulfilled since he was not learning as much as he hoped he would; he felt like he was only teaching. He wanted to make himself better by learning through experience, and he felt the job in Italy was not offering him that opportunity. For this reason, Malekai decided to leave this job and move to New York City.

He landed a job at Next Gen HQ, a hub that cultivates community, resources, and education to support the next generation of entrepreneurs and changemakers. Here, Malekai was in an environment where he would do three things: learn, learn, and learn. He was surrounded by people just like him: ambitious people who did not want corporate jobs and had a desire to tackle real-world problems. From these people—many of whom were actually younger than him—Malekai learned a great deal about entrepreneurship, helping other people, and making the world a better place. He was surrounded by knowledge that he would absorb through "doing." He would offer advice to entrepreneurs, make connections for other people, organize events, and much more. Just by seeing all of these young, ambitious individuals, Malekai learned, "you can always expand your horizons even further than you think." He also explains that he learned the importance of managing your time wisely and using it to the best of your ability. In other words, ensure that whatever you do with your time is aligned with your goals and dreams for the future. During our interview, Malekai did not even know where to start when talking about what Next Gen HQ has taught him. However, he does know these experiences were super fulfilling, not only because he is more prepared for future entrepreneurial endeavors but also because he has fun learning and meeting great people along the way.

Malekai stressed the importance of learning in any way at any stage in life. He suggested being an intern for someone you admire and learning what they are doing because "if you're not always learning, what are you doing?"

The experience of consistently learning is adding value to his personal life as well as his professional life. He is more fulfilled, and he is gaining more knowledge. However, these benefits do not only apply to Malekai.

While learning can be achieved in many ways, one of the most common methods is through reading. The benefits of reading educational content offer us a glimpse into the value of learning. You may be surprised to learn that, on top of the other positives, reading/learning also boosts our mental health. Studies show that those who read at least thirty minutes per week are 20 percent more likely to have greater life satisfaction, 11 percent more likely to feel creative, 18 percent more likely to have higher self-esteem, and 28 percent less likely to suffer from depression (Stillman 2015). It's thirty minutes a week—not even thirty minutes a day (which, by the way, is very doable). Such a small-time investment yields outstanding results, displaying the effects of learning and engaging the mind.

*

LEARNING AND TAKING CONTROL OF YOUR LIFE
Vedavyas Jampanaboyana (VJ) grew up in the suburbs of Pennsylvania after his parents immigrated to the United States from India. Just like most elementary school kids during this time, VJ was in love with Pokémon cards! Starting with a single pack of Pokémon cards, VJ traded his way up to an entire binder filled with a wide variety of cards. This mindset set the groundwork and foreshadowed VJ's future interest in business and entrepreneurship.

Toward the end of eighth grade, VJ was diagnosed with a rare condition called Crohn's disease. This is a disease that affects the lining of a person's digestive tract, and thus, it has had an enormous impact on VJ's life. As a competitive athlete, VJ was disappointed when he had to stop playing travel soccer due to Crohn's. In addition, his diet became limited because certain foods irritated his stomach. To add insult to injury, VJ was entering high school, which is not an easy transition. On top of the changing course load, social structure, and after-school activities, VJ now needed to manage this new disease that he was forced to live with.

At this time, VJ started to embody his elementary school self and tap back into his love for entrepreneurship. VJ watched movies that depicted Silicon Valley tycoons as influential entrepreneurs who had an impact on the world. He would read books and immerse himself in the world of entrepreneurship.

One thing, however, that really changed his life was when his high school sponsored a trip to an FBLA (Future Business Leader of America) conference. VJ attended this event and was shocked to see what he had walked into. He met inspiring individuals and speakers who had taken control of their lives and were now making the world a better place. Looking at the possibilities, the speakers had inspired VJ, and he was pretty impressed. Their potential was limitless, and they were taking on prominent issues in the world. VJ explained, "they were figuring out ways to take control of their obstacles instead of letting the obstacles take control of them." As someone who felt that his obstacle (namely, Crohn's disease) was taking control of his life, VJ immediately connected with these people and wanted to be a part of what they were doing—entrepreneurship.

"The kind of freedom of being an entrepreneur and being yourself is exciting," VJ pointed out. "I realized that I was letting this Crohn's drive my life instead of driving my life by myself and having this be a factor." Entrepreneurship was his way of taking control of his own life, and he was ready to learn more about this field!

VJ had one problem, though—he had little to no knowledge about business and entrepreneurship. Yes, he watched movies about large companies. Yes, he had attended an FBLA conference. Still, he was not prepared to enter the entrepreneurial world. He was lacking knowledge. So, what did he do to combat this issue? It's simple. He went out to learn. He connected with entrepreneurs and changemakers on Facebook and LinkedIn to speak with them and learn about their journeys. He also attended different conferences to network and met new faces. In fact, I actually met VJ at a conference two years before writing this book! He continued to learn (and still does) as much as he could because after Crohn's took his life for a spin, he "had to figure out how to manage and how to learn." In other words, for him to take control of his life by diving into the entrepreneurial space, he had to learn as much as he possibly could. To him, knowledge and, in turn, entrepreneurship meant taking control of his life.

After learning a great deal of information, VJ felt the responsibility to help others who are facing challenges and want to use entrepreneurship as a way of taking control of their lives. He and his cofounder started GIYLS, which stands for "Global Innovation and Youth Leaders Summit." Their goal is to "motivate youth into recognizing their own obstacles while pursuing social change through an entrepreneurial lens." He expressed that he was not always interested in creating an organization, but after learning so much and figuring out how to take control of his own life, VJ felt that establishing this organization and passing on this knowledge was the right thing to do.

According to the *Harvard Business Review*, constantly learning can delay symptoms of Alzheimer's and offset cognitive decline (Coleman 2017). That is taking control of your life. The same source explains that the mission to constantly learn allows you to build genuine relationships (both personally and professionally) since you will show genuine curiosity toward the other person. That is taking control of your life. A high school student diagnosed with Crohn's disease, thinking his life had hit a significant obstacle, had learned about entrepreneurship and encouraged others to bring about change. Now, that is *truly* taking control of your life.

*

TAKEAWAY

Far too often, people feel that once they become successful, they should stop learning. Even those who have not "made it" yet don't always see the value in experience, knowledge, and education. It is critical to understand that always learning allows you to take control of your own life and succeed even more because you can always learn something new. And to be clear, don't just learn something and sit on it; rather, you should learn something and do something with it. This can be by bettering your life or bettering someone else's life. By applying what you have learned, you not only make a difference, but you actually retain the information better. We only remember 10 percent of the information we read and a mere 5 percent of information given in the form of a lecture. Once we apply what we have learned to the real world, however, this retention rate skyrockets to 90 percent.

Learning has the ability to create wonders. And it isn't just me or the people I interviewed who believe this; rather, it is a phenomenon backed by evidence, data, and examples. Did you know that Shaquille O'Neal, the former professional basketball player, earned his PhD and MBA while playing for the Los Angeles Lakers? Shaq never stopped learning, and neither should you; because, as Mahatma Gandhi once said, "Live as if you were to die tomorrow. Learn as if you were to live forever."

PART 3

GO TIME

7

TAKING ACTION AND EXECUTING

"The only impossible journey is the one you never begin."
—TONY ROBBINS

In 2010, we moved out of our house, and the construction workers moved in as we had decided to renovate. It was falling apart, and we thought it would be a good idea for the house to get a "makeover." When the renovation was complete, there was still something that was out of place—the porch.

The porch was made of decrepit splintering wood, and to be honest, it was kind of dangerous to walk on it. It seemed obvious we would want that repaired along with the rest of our house. My father was in charge of the outside, while my mother was responsible for the inside of the house, so my father thought about the porch and whether to convert it into a patio. It was decided he was going to "think about it." Time went by, and life moved on. Every six to nine months, the idea of the new patio would be brought up, but my father still hadn't made a decision. Should we convert it into a patio or leave it as a porch? How much money should we spend? What kind of stones should we use? Thoughts and variables complicated the situation, and nothing progressed.

As I am sitting down and writing this, I am happy to announce that the patio has just been completed—ten years later! Yes, ten years—120 months; 520 weeks; 3,650 days; 87,000 hours; 5,256,000 minutes; 315,360,000 seconds. Whatever way you want to think about it, this was a long time to get a simple patio repaired.

So what's the point in telling this seemingly random story? This patio project took such a long time because my father was experiencing something called "analysis paralysis." As the name suggests, this is when you become "paralyzed" from analyzing too much. As James Chen mentions in an Investopedia article, "analysis paralysis refers to a situation in which an individual or group is unable to move forward with a decision as a result of overanalyzing data or overthinking a problem" (Chen 2021).

While it is definitely beneficial to think about your actions and not make rash decisions, overthinking can lead to problems since it does not allow you to move forward with anything. Thoughts in your head are great, but if you want to make them real, you must execute upon them and take action. This is what Kim Perell learned to be the most critical factor when it comes to success.

*

NEW ACTION AFTER FAILURE

Kim Perell was born in Portland, Oregon, to a middle-class family. She was not born with a silver spoon in her mouth. Rather, she was raised by two entrepreneurs who were constantly struggling to make ends meet. Her father owned an auto repair shop, which eventually went bust. He then shifted his focus to the food industry by opening up a restaurant. However, just like his auto repair shop, his restaurant went bust. Perell's father then decided to open up a bar, hoping it would be more profitable, but that hope proved to be in vain when this business went under as well.

At the dinner table, the family did not talk about sports and politics like most households; instead, they spoke about the hardships they were facing and how they would overcome them. Even though Kim did not realize it at the time, she was subconsciously absorbing life-changing business lessons that would serve her well into the future.

Upon completing high school, Kim attended Pepperdine University, where she not only earned a Bachelor of Science in Business Administration but also graduated magna cum laude. She had the desire to work in the tech industry, especially because the age of the internet was ramping up. Shortly after college, Kim landed her dream job as the Marketing Director at Xdrive, a fast-growing tech company. She convinced her friends and family members to invest in the company and work with her. Kim was convinced they would all become dot-com millionaires. She could not have been farther from the truth. The "dot-com bubble" burst (when the stock prices of many internet companies came crashing down), and so did the success of Xdrive. In her speech entitled "How to Execute and

Make Things Happen," Perell explained, "When Xdrive went bankrupt, it was the worst time in my life." She was forced to lay off friends, family members, and colleagues after promising them success. "I felt like such a failure," recalled Perell.

Kim felt that her career, income, future, and relationships had been deleted with the snap of a finger. She was scared because, for her, the future was uncertain. Reflecting back on this traumatizing experience, Perell pointed out, "Hitting rock bottom really makes you realize what you want in life, and I didn't want to be broke again." Obviously, her goal of not being broke again was easier said than done, but Perell made it her mission to find success.

Three months after the demise of Xdrive, Kim launched her own online marketing firm called Frontline Direct. To many, Kim was crazy for jumping back into the tech industry after she lost almost everything due to the "dot-com bubble." This did not stop Perell, who was in her early twenties at the time, from chasing her dream and pursuing her passions of technology and marketing. She had hit rock bottom, and the only way to go was up. She moved to Hawaii with her boyfriend and his family because she could live there rent-free. And while this may seem luxurious, it was not. She did not spend her time at the beach learning to hula dance and surfing in Hawaiian waters. Rather, she lived in a small and crowded apartment, trying to figure out her new marketing business.

She funded her new venture with $10,000 in the bank and a heaping load of credit card debt. While working on her business from the kitchen table, Kim was forced to listen to the other apartment residents playing MTV at blaring volumes. Her life has seemed to have taken a substantial downgrade. She went from the director of marketing at a multimillion-dollar tech firm to a broke individual working in a small and noisy apartment. Many people would have been discouraged by this sudden lifestyle change, but Perell did not let this setback hinder her future success.

She grew her company from the ground up, and it eventually reached $100 million in annual revenue. She successfully sold her company in 2014 for an astonishing $235 million. She wanted to pay it forward by investing in other start-ups, and she did precisely that by becoming an angel investor. She has invested in over seventy companies, dozens of which have sold for over $500 million. In fact, one of the start-ups she invested in had their IPO and sold for more than $1 billion on their first day. To say Kim turned her life around is an understatement. She went from broke college graduate not knowing what the future would hold to a successful entrepreneur who now invests in dozens of wildly successful companies.

Reflecting on her past success, Kim realizes this was possible due to one crucial factor: execution. Perell shines a light on the reality that "an idea is only as good as how well you can execute it." Perell breaks down the concept of execution into five main steps: vision, passion, action, resilience, and relationships.

VISION
"Vision is about having a North Star," explained Perell. It's hard to get to where you want to be in life if you're not even sure where that is. Imagine driving a car to a destination,

but you don't know what the destination is. Do you think you will ever get there? Knowing what you want to achieve will increase your chances of reaching those goals since you will have a sense of direction. On a piece of paper, Kim wrote down that she wanted to sell her company by June 2014. And guess what? She sold her company in June of 2014. Have a destination because that is what's going to guide you to your dreams.

PASSION

"What is something that you are so passionate about that you would gladly suffer for?" asked Kim. You must be emotionally attached to your goals because you will be willing to put in the blood, sweat, and tears to make your vision a reality. As a child, Kim loved horseback riding, but her parents could not afford lessons. She made a deal with the stable that for every seven hours of work she did (which mostly entailed her cleaning up poop), she would get a one-hour lesson in return. She was passionate about horseback riding, and she was willing to put in the time to reap the benefits. Work is not work if you enjoy it.

ACTION

Kim offered some great advice when she said, "You have to be willing to take that first step, and it doesn't have to be right." Taking that first step is the hardest step you will take, but it is essential to reaching your goals. Take action, even if it may seem that you are not ready or you are wrong. I'll be honest; chances are something will go wrong, but that is life. You need to get up, dust the dirt off of your pants, and keep going.

RESILIENCE

This is such an essential trait because, as Mike Tyson once said, "Everyone has a plan until they get punched in the face." In other words, nothing ever goes as planned, which is why it is paramount to be ready for failure and disappointment so you can fight it later on. Think about potential obstacles in the future because, this way, you will be more prepared for them. Getting up after being knocked down is easier said than done, but the sooner you understand the importance of resilience, or more importantly, the sooner you incorporate resilience into your life, the sooner you will find success.

RELATIONSHIPS

"Nobody is successful alone," stated Kim. People will support you along your journey, and it is important to value those relationships. Perell recommends performing a "life audit" once a year, which is where you figure out who is supporting you and who is dragging you down. In other words, who is making a positive impact on your life and who is having a negative effect. Further your relationships with those who help you with your dreams and cut the toxic people out of your life. Genuine relationships not only benefit you in business—but also in life.

You can learn to execute on your goals and ambitions with visions, passion, action, resilience, and relationships. An idea is simply an idea until you take action and build upon it. Ideas are worthless unless you do something with them. Through the life experiences and lessons of Kim Perell, it becomes apparent that execution is the driving force of success. Because, if you try but don't find success the first time, nothing says you won't find it the second time!

A survey found that, on average, employees spend more than half of their time receiving and managing information instead of using it (Kane). In other words, they are looking at the information and thinking about what to do with it, but most of the time, they're not actually doing it! "Most folks waste time muddling in fear and overthinking all the what-ifs," pointed out Bedros Keuilian in an Entrepreneur.com article, and this mentality can be and often is paralyzing. This is problematic because, as Keuilian puts it, "It's true in business and in life that if you move slowly, you lose" (Keuilian 2019). It seems counterintuitive because it would make sense that the more you plan something out, the better the result will be. However, this is not true. The reality of the situation is that if you spend too much time planning and little time executing the plan, the result can turn out to be horrible.

"Analysis paralysis" has many causes, but one of the main ones is the fear of taking action and the fear of doing something wrong. An idea is an idea in your head, but once you execute upon it, it is real, and this can be scary. I know this because I felt the same way when it came to writing this very book!

*

THIS BOOK'S JOURNEY
When I was in tenth grade and interested in business/entrepreneurship, I was eager to learn more about this field and how to get involved. I would reach out to entrepreneurs on LinkedIn, Facebook, email, and text to have a conversation with them and learn more about what they did. I wanted to hear about their experiences, what they learned, and any

advice they had for me. When the COVID-19 pandemic hit, I continued on with this activity and constantly had phone calls so that I could learn more. I had more time on my hands because many of my after-school activities were canceled. I wanted to use this time to engage in something I was interested in—entrepreneurship. The knowledge I gained inspired me to write a book so others could learn as well.

As of April 2020, my dream was set: I was going to write a book. This felt like it could be a massively advantageous experience for me because I would be able to learn even more—and additionally, I could even teach others about young entrepreneurs and how they overcome roadblocks. I had heard about other people writing books, so why not me? I had the idea in my head to write a book, but it was just an idea.

And it stayed an idea for quite a long time. To be honest, having the idea to write the book felt like that's all I needed to do. I had an idea, and I was proud of that. So I simply thought about what my book was going to be about. August of 2020 rolled around quicker than I expected, and I was still at the same spot with my book as I had been in April. It was still just an idea in my head.

I finally found a program that was able to mentor me and teach me how to write a book as a first-time author. After joining the program, I had the same sense of accomplishment that I had when I came up with the idea to write a book. I felt that joining the program was good enough. But now I had to do work? What is this?

It was hard for me to actually do the work not only because I had a limited amount of time but also because I was scared of taking action. As soon as I took action and executed my idea, this project would become a reality, and that scared me to my core. I had more fears than all the paper in the world could hold. I'll list a few below.

- What would others think of me for writing a book?

- Would they think I'm crazy because I'm in high school?

- Will people make fun of me?

- What if my friends and family think the book is bad?

- What if no one buys my book?

- What if I am embarrassed after releasing the book?

- Will my classmates make fun of the fact that I wrote a book at a young age?

- What if people see me as a failure because it is not a well-written piece of literature?

These thoughts paralyzed me. To cope with these thoughts, I simply did not do the work, and my progress came to a halt. My fellow authors were writing thousands of words, posting on social media, talking to colleagues, and being confident while I sat on my couch watching Netflix because I was scared I would mess something up in the book-writing journey. I wasn't taking action or executing; instead, I took the easier way out because it was the most comfortable.

Around the end of November, the leader of this program reminded us that we needed to turn in twenty thousand words of content in the next six weeks, so they could make sure we were on track. Uh-oh, I had zero words. My fear had paralyzed me and prevented me from taking action. I was so worried about what others would think and whether the book would be a success—that I didn't write anything. I had two options at this point. Do I work really hard over the next couple of weeks to interview people and write twenty thousand words, or do I give up and say this isn't for me? That was a difficult question to answer, but an easier one to think about was:

What will I regret more?

1. Writing a book to the best of my ability after learning so much about entrepreneurship and having some people laugh at me for my ambition.

or

2. Giving up and letting my passion for entrepreneurship be washed away simply because I cared so much about what others thought.

I would regret giving up, and that was my fuel to push forward. I interviewed dozens of people, researched statistics, and wrote tens of thousands of words. And now, the book I was once afraid of writing is in your hands!

Taking action with this book was not easy, and I could have avoided all my fears by simply giving up, but do you know what else I would have avoided by giving up? I would've avoided my dream of writing a book.

I was scared to take action, and this mentality hindered my progress and affected me personally. Numerous studies have shown that overthinking while not taking action disrupts sleep patterns and leads to changes in appetite (Ries 2020). Being passive and not taking action often seems like the easier route; however, it is often the most detrimental option in the long run. Utilizing brain scans, researchers at Stanford University found those who tended to overthink situations were less creative than their counterparts (Tank 2020). This shows that taking action (the opposite of overthinking) often leads to creativity and, thus, success in business. Take it from Atisha Patel, who learned the value of execution after implanting her idea into the real world.

*

THROWING YOUR IDEA INTO THE WORLD

Atisha Patel grew up in South Jersey. As a child, she was exposed to the idea of hustling, working hard, and taking part in numerous endeavors from her Indian parents. Even though both of her parents had full-time jobs, she noticed that they were always doing something else—such as investing in a motel or starting a business with another family. For Atisha, seeing this as a child normalized having multiple passions and endeavors at the same time. Little did she know, the seed of entrepreneurship was being planted into her head. The notion of working small jobs whenever the opportunity arose began making its way into Atisha's life when she was in college.

"When I was in college, I'd want to do small jobs here and there, not because I had to but because that's what I knew," she explained during our interview. "I didn't know any better in a sense, and that was a good thing." Atisha attended Drexel University in Philadelphia, and afterward, she worked in biomedical engineering for Big Pharma for over a decade.

Atisha made it a habit to go out to the bars with her now-cofounder every Wednesday. They would sit down, order a couple of martinis, and talk about how they were going to change the world. After some time, they got onto the topic of the medical field and the interactions between healthcare providers and the families of patients. They saw how these parents and families were struggling mentally and emotionally because they did now know what was happening with their loved ones in the hospital without visiting them in person. As a result, families would call the doctors and nurses to ask for an update. However, this constant calling from different families began to disrupt the workflow of healthcare providers. Atisha knew this was inefficient, and there could be a way to make this communication easier.

Entrepreneurship is not something Atisha thought consciously about as a child. Still, she was an engineer, so naturally, she wanted to figure out the solution whenever she saw a problem. In many ways, the entrepreneurial traits that she developed stemmed from her expertise in engineering. She and her cofounder began to brainstorm ideas at the bar and eventually came up with NotiCare (which was shorthand for "notifications for your cared ones.") This would be the platform that bridges the communication gap between healthcare providers and the patient's family by sending them live updates. Even though Atisha and her cofounder were excited about the business, there was a problem. Atisha was an engineer-in-training, and her cofounder was in finance and knew nothing about entrepreneurship either. This would be a challenge, and "it was a completely new learning curve" for both of them.

What they did when they left the bar sounds crazy. Two individuals who knew little about entrepreneurship settled on their idea, went home, purchased a domain name, wrote out a business plan, and began creating the business! Remember, this was still Wednesday, the same day they went to the bar, had some drinks, and chatted. This phase of a company's development usually takes longer than one night for most people, but Atisha and her partner moved at a *rapid* pace.

"We were just like let's try it and throw this idea to doctors and nurses and see what they say," described Atisha. They knew their platform would not be perfect right off the bat, but they understood they needed to take the first steps if they wanted a chance of succeeding. They proceeded at a breakneck pace. Atisha made a salient point about this newfound momentum, saying, "Because it was not our livelihood, that was the reason we were able to execute quicker." Atisha nor her cofounder quit their day job, and as a result, they had a backup plan if NotiCare failed. This allowed them to take more risks and get the ball rolling at a faster pace. "When you have security, you are more prone to take a risk," said Atisha.

Atisha recommends sticking with your day job when starting a business so you have something to fall back on. This pushes you to take risks and execute because you know the worst-case scenario is that you return to your life before the business. As your business begins to expand, you may need to alter your strategy. But, to start off, Atisha recommends that you ease into entrepreneurship rather than jumping into the deep end altogether.

Atisha has enjoyed much success in her business, which shows that her strategy of keeping her day job and executing quickly on ideas has served her quite well.

*

TAKEAWAY

So how can we fight the monster of overthinking? Believe it or not, the most powerful way to fight "analysis paralysis" is to recognize its existence and understand its consequences. This sounds crazy, but it is true. Now that you know how dangerous this phenomenon can be, hopefully, you will try your best to avoid it and execute ideas quicker. If you didn't realize that overthinking was detrimental, why would you stop doing it at all? I know this probably was not the solution you were looking for, but it is vital to understand and remember the consequences of overthinking so you can avoid it in the future. That being said, there is one thing you can start doing today that will force you to take action.

Write your goals on a piece of paper and tape it to a wall or mirror that you see every day. This constant reminder encourages you to take action and achieve your dreams rather than simply waiting. In fact, you are 42 percent more likely to achieve your goals if you write them down (Forleo 2019).

Now, by no means am I saying you should run out and make random, rash decisions. Instead, I'm expressing that overthinking details can lead to negative results and that trusting yourself and executing upon your idea is often the best choice. As Chris Sacca—venture investor and billionaire—points out, "Ideas are cheap. Execution is everything." By not taking action, you may avoid failure in its most traditional definition. But, by not taking action, you avoid success by every definition.

8

THE BEST TIME TO START IS NOW

―

"Only put off until tomorrow what you are willing to die having left undone"

—PABLO PICASSO

Have you ever found yourself under a looming deadline, and you just can't seem to do anything? Procrastination is natural. I do it, you do it, we all do it. When there is a big project or a daunting task, it is easy to put it off until another time. The justification is likely something along the lines of, "I still have a lot of time," or "I will be more prepared to do it later on," or "I work best when I am under pressure." This habit, which is often applied to projects or tasks around the house, can also make its way into the more prominent aspects of your life. This is where procrastination meets entrepreneurship.

Similar to procrastination, it is natural to want to wait until you are older to embark on your entrepreneurial journeys.

You may think that when you are older, you are more likely to become successful, and this may be true, but that should not stop you from starting a venture at a young age. Being young has many benefits you should take advantage of when it comes to entrepreneurship, including (but not limited to) reduced risk and fewer responsibilities. Starting a business or a venture at a young age is not easy, but that should not deter you from trying. Through his journey, Shreyas Parab learned the importance of starting young and how his age was a benefit as opposed to a liability.

*

TEENAGE TIE TYCOON

When you think of a typical ninth-grader, what comes to your mind? Someone hanging out with their friends? Someone playing baseball? Someone watching TV or playing video games? All of these are valid responses given how most "traditional" teenagers spend their time. Shreyas Parab is different. Shreyas grew up in Delaware. When he was in ninth grade, he "did possibly the most ridiculous and unheard-of thing a ninth-grader could do at the time. [He] started a tie company." Yes, you read that right; a fourteen-year-old freshman in high school started his very own clothing line.

When Shreyas was in high school, he had to wear a tie as a part of his uniform, and he hated it. This was no exception for his classmates and peers who weren't in love with the fabric wrapped around their necks. That's when the lightbulb went off in Shreyas's head. Why couldn't there be ties that were fun to wear; ties that would make formal events fun; ties that would be conversation pieces? There is no reason why that couldn't be the case! Shreyas wanted to solve this problem for himself and his classmates by creating this tie company. The problem was, he was young and had little to no experience or knowledge of entrepreneurship.

Shreyas provided a peek into his mindset at the time, stating, "I thought that I would have to wait for an adult to give their approval or give me the green light, but what I realized was as kids, we don't need a green light, we can go ahead and do it." And no, he does not mean literally not waiting for a green light and running a red light on the street. Instead, he means there is no reason why young people cannot enter the business world and make an impact on the planet. Shreyas took his own advice and went out to start his tie company: NovelTie. The purpose was to create fun and creative ties that you would actually want to wear and show off, rather than ones you would feel forced to don.

Since he did not know how to start and run a tie company, he had to figure it out with the help of other people. "This isn't something they really teach you at school," said Shreyas. "I had to reach out to every person I knew for advice, help, and guidance, and just talk to them about what I was doing, and I was surprisingly shocked to see how many people out there were willing to help me." Being a young entrepreneur is not as easy as it sounds; in fact, it comes with many challenges. But it also has many benefits.

He explained, "[The company] is one of the most difficult and challenging things I have ever had to do, but it is also the most fun, the most exciting, and the one I love doing the most." Through the obstacles Shreyas has faced, he realized that being a kid was actually an advantage and, in many ways, a superpower. People were able to help him out and offer him advice due to his young age and because they were once in his position. Shreyas encourages young entrepreneurs and changemakers to ask for assistance since there are so many people out there willing to offer you a helping hand. He learned as much as he could from friends, family, and connections he had made through cold emailing.

Furthermore, being young is an advantage because you have low liability. "When you become an adult, you have to worry about your mortgage, your 401(k), paying taxes, but as a kid, you have the time and the drive to explore your passions," explained Shreyas. As a kid, you can afford to fail because it will be a learning opportunity for your next venture. This way, you won't make the same mistake in a situation where a higher stake is involved. As a kid, there is little risk, so why not give it a shot? Obviously, this is easier said than done, but the reality is: you have a low liability when you're young. Thus, failure is an option—and you will learn from those experiences.

Today, NovelTie makes around $75,000 in annual sales. And while this did not turn into a billion-dollar company, "NovelTie has changed my life," explained Shreyas. This company has opened up a myriad of doors for the young entrepreneur. He was able to donate money to schools and entrepreneurship programs. He was able to meet with CEOs of Fortune 500 companies. He was able to give one of his ties to Joe Biden! This company, this project, this "longshot" has allowed Shreyas to work with billionaires and apply his knowledge in other fields of business. In fact, Shreyas started an education company that had a successful exit during his junior year of high school.

Now, Shreyas attends Stanford University, and continues to work on his passions as he is an investment partner at Dorm Room Fund, a venture capital firm focused on student-run start-ups. From his experiences as a young entrepreneur and changemaker, Shreyas has learned and understands the power of being young. Far too often, people view youth as a disadvantage in the business world, but Shreyas begs to differ. Especially when you are young, give your goals a shot because if they succeed, great! But if they don't, great! Why is that great? Because you will have learned something that can be applied to your next effort, bringing you that much closer to where you want to be. Shreyas concludes his message by saying, "Write the story that you want to read."

Like Shreyas mentioned, when you are younger, you have fewer bills to pay and fewer responsibilities to manage. This is evident when taking a look at the average debt that people have. Individuals between the ages of eighteen and twenty-three have an average debt balance of $9,593, people between the ages of twenty-four and thirty-nine have a balance of $78,398, and people from the ages of forty to fifty-five owe $135,841 (DeMatteo 2021). It is more than clear that, overall, the younger generation has less debt (they are younger, so this makes sense). Thus, this indicates that, for the most part, they have fewer responsibilities. This is hugely beneficial because it allows you to take on more risks and experiment with new ideas; after all, you don't really have anything to lose.

Alexandra Twin elaborates on this idea in an Investopedia article, "Risk tolerance is often associated with age [...] people who are younger and have a longer time horizon are often able to and are encouraged to take on greater risk than people older with a shorter-term horizon" (Twin 2020). To add to this, a Medium article entitled "What Are the Benefits of Being a Young Entrepreneur?" points out that younger people "are much more likely to take risks which ultimately lead to success" (MUNPlanet 2017). If you start a business in high school or college, and it fails, the result most likely won't be devastating. On the other hand, if you are older, have a mortgage to pay, credit card debt, utility bills, food to put on the table, and healthcare expenses—a failing business will be a much larger problem. Use your young age to your advantage by taking on more risks and experimenting.

Being young in the start-up space has more benefits than just risk tolerance. A prime example of this is Jesse Kay, who tapped into the power of his youth to find success.

*

TEENAGE PODCASTER
Jesse Kay grew up in New Jersey, and ever since he was nine years old, he has dealt with panic attacks and anxiety all the way to the point where he didn't want to go to school. He explained that he was highly anxious. He said he "was the kid who got picked up at 11:50 from a friend's house." He even had trouble sleeping at his grandparents' house! For most, this nervous and anxious stage of life generally ends at around eight or nine years old, but for Jesse, he was like this until he

was sixteen. He looked for an outlet to deal with his anxiety. Interested in business, entrepreneurship, and money, Jesse spent his childhood flipping sneakers on eBay. He would buy them for a low price, wait for them to become more valuable, then sell them and pocket the money.

As successful as he was at flipping sneakers, Jesse felt he had bigger fish to fry. At the age of sixteen, he started the *20 Under 20s* podcast to inspire the next generation of entrepreneurs and leaders. Hoping to create an impactful and influential podcast, Jesse aimed to bring successful entrepreneurs, changemakers, and leaders onto his show so they could share their experiences and offer some advice for the future. There was only one problem with this otherwise creative idea: he did not know anyone to interview! Yeah, that would be a problem considering the fact that this podcast relied on conversations with successful individuals.

At this point, many teenagers would have given up on their idea and focused more on playing sports, hanging out with friends, or watching Netflix. But in case you haven't gathered yet, Jesse was different. He wanted to learn more about entrepreneurship and business as well as educate other teens on these topics. Jesse has always had a passion for this subject and was not going to let one (what seemed like impossible to overcome) hurdle get in his way. Unfortunately, the tenacious teenager quickly realized he not only lacked connections but also that people would not take him seriously because of his young age. Plus, successful individuals did not want to be on a podcast without a large audience and an established reputation. To others, this endeavor seemed beyond possible, but to Jesse, this was just the beginning.

He did something that many of us are afraid to do. He did something that is far too often frowned upon. He did something that wasn't easy. He cold emailed. Yes, he reached out to people he had not talked to before and asked them if they would be a guest on his podcast. He sent out 350 emails per day for four months! That's over forty-two thousand emails! He leveraged his youth and changed his subject line of emails from "Podcast interview" to "Sixteen-year-old podcast interview." In his speech entitled "Business Is for Teenagers Too," Jesse explains that people began responding, and it showed in the numbers. His email open rate went from 20 to 95 percent. He began interviewing them, and the podcast gained traction. As a result, more people were willing to join him in the podcast, and more people tuned in to hear the valuable insights he was going to bring.

Jesse has interviewed a wide array of people, from professional athletes including Mikey Taylor and Trevor Bookers to successful entrepreneurs such as Grant Cardone, Gary Vaynerchuck, and Jeff Hoffman. According to his speech, in eleven months, Jesse went from an idea to an established podcast with over one hundred thousand downloads. He was not sure whether his podcast was going to be a household name or if it was going to crash and burn after its launch, but one thing he did know was he was going to give it a shot. Jesse drove this message home when he explained, "99 percent of the time, you think you have the idea, and that's where it ends. You need to be that 1 percent that says 'I like this idea, why don't I try it out, there's nothing to lose.'"

If you fail, if it does not bring in millions of dollars, if it did not follow the path you envisioned, you will learn from your mistakes and experiences. You will never taste success if you aren't willing to throw your hat in the ring and give it a shot. Jesse went from an anxious teenager to one of the most successful young entrepreneurs because he was willing to give his goals a chance, and he was willing to take the risk. Had he failed, he would have learned, moved on, and applied these lessons to his next venture.

Today, Jesse is the host of the *Trendsetters* podcast, a platform aiming to provide entrepreneurial content to Generation Z. He is the CEO of Vyber Media, a digital consulting agency that helps Fortune 500 businesses and athletes connect with customers and monetize their relationships through social media. Furthermore, Jesse has raised over $100,000 for COVID-19 relief. These accomplishments are just the tip of the iceberg for his future. Instead of doubting himself and waiting for the "perfect" time to chase his dreams, he is willing to take a chance and go for it. There is *never* a "perfect" time to achieve your goals, and if you leave them on the back burner, they will stay on the back burner. Jesse continued to encourage other young entrepreneurs by saying, "Don't wait; start today."

Chris Ronzio of Inc.com outlines the benefits of starting a business at a young age, and one of their key points is, "You're already under-promising" (Ronzio 2018). In other words, at a young age, people don't expect you to be this genius who can start and manage a company perfectly. They already have low expectations of you. You may see this as a bad thing, but take a look at it on the bright side. When others have low expectations of you, and you perform really well, they will be impressed and delighted. Use this to your advantage. Embrace their preconceived notion that you are incapable of many things, and then show them your talents. This will open up more doors and lead to grander opportunities. Also, Ronzio pointed out, "Students get meetings" (Ronzio 2018). This basically means people will be impressed with your young age and thus will be more likely to meet with you and help you. This is evident in the story of Jesse Kay, where people were eager to meet and help him due to his youth. Tapping into your young age and using this to your advantage reaps a myriad of benefits.

Starting young also gives you more time to learn. As you know, learning is so important, and engaging in entrepreneurship at a young age simply gives you more time to gain knowledge and explore your interests. Aditya Desai, who began his entrepreneurial journey in high school, realized how much of a learning experience it was and how it might not have been possible if he waited until he was older.

*

TEENAGE TEACHER
Aditya Desai was born and raised in New Jersey. His parents indirectly pushed him toward the entrepreneurial path. His mother, a doctor, decided not to join a large medical group as many of her peers did. Instead, she decided to start and run her own practice. In addition, Aditya's father works in the liquor space, runs his own retail stores, and manages some online ventures. Seeing their work ethic and what their lifestyle was like, influenced Aditya to pursue entrepreneurship and make an impact on the world. Aditya points out that his parents' experiences have "been a huge factor in allowing me to believe that it's possible to be an entrepreneur."

When Aditya was a freshman in high school, he earned an internship in Long Island. The goal of this project was to research and eventually offer potential solutions to health-related issues. What Aditya did first was conduct some research. He talked to people in the greater New York area and asked them questions to learn more about their situations. One scenario Aditya posed was, "If you only have enough money to buy the prescription drugs that you need or a new pair of Jordan shoes, which do you buy?" Aditya assumed a vast majority of people would say the medication, but he was in for a shock. He found that a large portion of people would rather buy the new pair of sneakers as opposed to the medication they needed. This surprised Aditya. "That kind of showed me that people don't have the financial literacy that I suppose they do, and maybe this is a larger problem," explained Aditya. This inspired him to tackle the issue of financial illiteracy and help people make the best decisions with their money.

Initially, he wanted to do some work on the side to address this problem, but he never thought creating an actual organization was within his capabilities. Even if he did ever think of a potential organization, he did not believe the potential organization could get funding or "attract the attention of sponsors or entrepreneurs." So he simply started working with students in low-income communities. He developed courses and taught them key concepts such as economics, investing, budgeting, etc.

This endeavor picked up a great deal of traction as Aditya helped hundreds of students. He even began to receive grants. That is when he knew he should take this "side project" to the next level so that people could get the financial education they needed. He launched the Economics Education Initiative (EEI), which offered financial literacy workshops, designed thinking summits, and hands-on experiences to develop entrepreneurial skills. In fact, the students took a trip to New York City and brainstormed ideas for a better way to navigate Penn Station. In addition, the EEI partnered with Scholastic and launched a magazine to feature successful young entrepreneurs. "Students can look up to them [the successful entrepreneurs] and contact them if they want," stated Aditya.

Aditya explained that starting this venture at a young age (high school) offered many benefits. But there were two, in particular, that seemed to be the most important. One was the ability to connect with the students who were his age. To an extent, he could understand what they were going through. He could understand their interests and used this to keep them engaged by creating custom simulations and experiences that they would enjoy. His young age allowed him "to empathize with the students on a more personal level," which allowed him to help them even more. The second benefit that Aditya pointed out was the fact that he could learn so much himself. It seems ironic since he was teaching others, but the reality is, Aditya learned a great deal about entrepreneurship. He learned about things he would not be able to learn through a textbook. Aditya said it perfectly, "If you learn when you're in the moment when you're actually at the activity, you might fail a couple of times, but when you get that experience, you're armed with that confidence [to succeed later on]."

Aditya is currently a senior in high school and will be attending the University of Pennsylvania (Wharton) next year. In the future, he first wants to tackle college. He hopes to "experiment with a lot of different things" and gain experience and expertise in many fields. This includes banking, consulting, venture capital, entrepreneurship, and other components of the business world. After college, he hopes to pursue these fields professionally. The benefits that Aditya reaped by engaging in entrepreneurship at a young age will provide him with a leg up, no matter what he chooses to do in life.

*

TAKEAWAY

"When young people fail, they have much more time to learn and reboot," notes an article from Medium, entitled "What Are the Benefits of Being a Young Entrepreneur?" (MUNPlanet 2017). This goes hand in hand with the BBC's findings, detailing that "University of Oxford scientists say that adults may find learning more difficult than children because their brains store memories differently." In other words, younger people find it easier to learn, and there is a slew of lessons one can learn from entrepreneurship. This may include critical thinking, adversity, independence, creativity, management, connections/networking, personal branding, and so on. Starting out young provides you with the opportunity to learn valuable skills that will be useful later down the road.

I am not sure how else to put it other than this: Start now. Because the longer you wait, the more opportunities will pass you by.

9

THE IMPORTANCE OF COMMUNITY

"You are the average of the five people you spend the most time with."

—JIM ROHN (ENTREPRENEUR)

Tell me if this story sounds familiar to you. An individual is tired of their traditional nine-to-five job, and they decide to start a business so they can take control of their own life. They quit the job they hate. To avoid all distractions, they lock themselves in their room for sixteen hours a day for two years without communicating with friends or family. They work really hard on their business, and after two years have passed, they emerge as millionaires!

Okay, this story may sound a little extreme, but the idea of becoming an entrepreneur by yourself and without support is one that many of us believe. It has been portrayed in various types of media that you can become successful and change the world without anyone else's help. This could not be farther from the truth. You are going to need help, support, and a community because these essential factors will help you achieve your goals.

*

LOCATION, LOCATION, LOCATION

Alex Mesmej was born and raised in Paris, France, to a middle-class family. He was interested in technology. "I was just fascinated with Steve Jobs," explained Alex. He would constantly read about Steve Jobs and Apple. Not only did Alex skip a grade (making him the youngest in his class), but he was an ambitious and optimistic kid who had big dreams. His classmates thought he was crazy for being an outcast, and thus he "was an easy target for bullies." Even though "they basically rejected" him, Alex still "would wear colorful clothes" because he accepted the fact that he was different—and he planned on using that to his advantage.

As his school years progressed, Alex's love and passion for technology continued to compound. He had "extreme, extreme ambition" and the mentality that "technology and building products is the best thing you can do with your life." He learned more about technology (even though he did not know how to code) and continued exploring different aspects of the industry.

When he turned eighteen, his parents sent him to the United Kingdom to continue his educational journey. In college, he learned a great deal about business and entrepreneurship.

However, Alex said the most valuable component of this experience was learning how to speak better English. This way, Alex could communicate with even more people, especially internationally, which would in turn help with his business career. Overall, this college experience allowed Alex to learn more about the world and what he wanted to do in the future. Alex explained, "I was just learning the theory of entrepreneurship."

After he completed college, he stayed in the UK to work on a start-up. Unfortunately, it was clear this business was not going to work out, and it went under rather quickly. On the bright side, Alex learned a lot about business management and operation, and these skills would benefit him down the line. Because his start-up failed, and he was not making money in the UK, his parents made him come back to France to live with them.

Just like during his childhood, Alex found he did not have an environment that supported his ambitions and dreams. "I couldn't find people who were like me," stated Alex. He felt he had taken a step backward, going from an environment in the UK where people supported his goals back to a place where he felt there was little support. Alex felt he was in a community that did not push him and inspire him to grow. That is when Alex said to himself, "I need to meet the best people ever." He wanted to find a community of ambitious individuals who were making an impact on the world so he could get to know them, learn from them, and earn their support.

Although he had trouble meeting like-minded people initially, Alex continued to network and meet as many people as possible through workshops and online events. Through mutual connections, Alex eventually met Xavier Niel, a French billionaire. After Xavier saw what an ambitious individual Alex was, Xavier invited him to apply for his program in the Bay Area (California). Xavier ran a school-like program in the Bay Area where students could learn about entrepreneurship, gain real-life experience, and meet like-minded people. Here is the thing: the program was completely free, and living expenses were covered! Alex became very excited because he was into technology, so the Bay Area would be perfect for him. Plus, he would be able to meet others who have similar interests to him. Alex applied, was accepted, and moved to the Bay Area to start the next chapter of his life.

Alex met countless friends who were just as ambitious and excited as he was, which was just what Alex wanted and needed. After a couple of months in this supportive environment, Alex became interested in crypto technology. He spent time with people in this space, went to conferences, networked, and learned a great deal about this industry and this type of technology. Later on, with his knowledge and supportive community, Alex was able to raise large sums of money for his projects.

This is not where it ended. Alex began to use Twitter to meet other people and learn from them. He would write content about crypto-technology, and through this, he would find people who were genuinely interested in what he was doing, and then he would learn from them. He described this process as "osmosis." It's a funny way of putting it, but it's true. If you surround yourself with ambitious people who know what they are doing, you will learn as well!

With his connections and experience, Alex started Showtime, a social media platform that uses crypto-technology to showcase digital art and eventually sell the art to customers. Its tagline reads, "Discover and showcase digital art." Alex is running with this idea, hiring people, and finding investors so this concept can have the most substantial impact possible on the world. Alex is living proof that the right community and support network can make all the difference in the world.

It is incredible to see how much of an influence your environment has on who you are. A study published in *Psychology Today* found that people with low self-control benefit from befriending disciplined individuals because it boosts the willpower of the person with low self-control (Morin 2015). To put it simply, the traits and attributes of your disciplined friends begin to rub off on you; and you, in turn, become more disciplined yourself.

Author Karen Marie Moning pointed out, "Who and what we surround ourselves with is who and what we become (Bonnell 2019). In the midst of good people, it is easy to be good. In the midst of bad people, it is easy to be bad." This goes back to the quote at the beginning of the chapter concerning how you are the average of the five people you spend the most time with. If you are spending your time with negative people who make you feel like your goals are silly, you will start to feel this way, too. On the other hand, if you surround yourself with encouraging and supportive people, I am sure you can imagine who you will become.

Being in an environment with supportive and like-minded individuals is not only beneficial mentally but also practically. This can be evidenced by my personal experiences as a fourteen-year-old interested in entrepreneurship.

NEXT GEN

The summer after my eighth-grade school year, I was becoming increasingly interested in entrepreneurship and change-making. I wanted to go to a conference that brought entrepreneurs together so I could network with them and learn as much as I could. Not only this, but I was looking forward to hearing from keynote speakers and learning from them as well. So I began the internet search for conferences I could attend. I found a bunch that looked really interesting and promising until I looked at the price. The tickets to these conferences cost thousands (and sometimes tens of thousands) of dollars. As a recent graduate of middle school, I did not have that type of money. So, what did I do? I asked my parents—and the conversation went something like this:

Me: "I found an entrepreneurship conference in California this summer! Can I go?"

Parents: "California? That's a bit far. Do you really want to go across the country?"

Me: "Yes."

Parents: "Okay! Well, how much will it cost?"

Me: "Somewhere between $10,000 and $15,000."

Parents: "Let's see if we can find a different conference."

So, I was back to square one, looking for affordable conferences. I found one called Next Gen Summit in New York City, and it looked great because it was built for the next generation of entrepreneurs. Most of the people who attended the conference were in college or had just graduated, so I was a bit younger than them. Still, I was closer in age to the attendees in the conference in New York than I would have been if I had gone to the one in California. I was really excited, and then I looked at the date of the conference. I had missed it—it was the weekend before! This was upsetting because I had finally found a conference that was affordable and the perfect fit for me, and now I couldn't go (unless I had a time machine).

I hopped on a call with someone from Next Gen to introduce myself. They encouraged me to come to the conference the following year and, in the meantime, to join their community on Facebook. So that is what I did. After being disappointed about not being able to travel across the country for an expensive conference and missing the affordable one, it turned out for the best—because I was able to join an amazing community that supported me, no matter where my dream took me.

I did end up attending the conference at the end of my freshman year (one year later). I met so many people and gained a great deal of knowledge. I did not know I could learn that much in a weekend! I also attended the virtual conference at the end of my sophomore year and had a blast there as well. Even when I was not at the in-person events, the community constantly helped me.

They helped me develop my business club in high school by connecting me with guest speakers and offering suggestions on how to attract more people. I have been able to find internship opportunities through the network, which has allowed me to gain knowledge, expertise, and experience in the start-up space. Believe it or not, many of the stories you are reading in this book are of people I met in the Next Gen community. My point is that this community/network has supported me with my entrepreneurial endeavors and offered assistance at every roadblock I have hit.

Ali Mirza, a contributor to the *Huffington Post*, once said, "No great entrepreneur of the past has ever succeeded without feedback and support" (van Doorn 2018). I know this has been evidenced in my life, considering it is difficult to imagine where I would be today if it wasn't for such a fantastic community like Next Gen. Having a network of supporters who can help you along the way is beneficial in countless ways, but don't just take it from me. Take it from Dwayne Griffith, who developed his network and tapped into making a difference in the world.

*

CREATING CONNECTIONS TO GET *AND* GIVE HELP
Dwayne Griffith was born on the island of Antigua. When he was just four months old, he and his twenty-two-year-old mother moved to St. Martin. Dwayne's mother was having financial troubles. When she went out looking for work and ways to make money, the neighbors took care of young Dwayne. Eventually, these neighbors officially adopted Dwayne because his mother could not afford to take care of him. This being said, Dwayne and his mother were still able

to keep a strong relationship because they would see each other on the weekends.

Dwayne's adoptive parents believed that the best course of action was for Dwayne to go to high school, get a job, and make money. Dwayne noted that they did not put an emphasis on college or finding passions; instead, they encouraged working traditional jobs. As a result, from fifth grade onward, Dwayne worked for one of the family member's businesses as a locksmith. "I would do a lot of customer service there," pointed out Dwayne. He would take customer orders, cut keys, and program electronic keys. He started to develop his entrepreneurial spirit here. As time progressed, however, Dwayne began to have a hard time. He found the business to be a toxic work environment because he was not respected when he came up with new ideas on how to improve the business. The older employees and owners—who were also his adoptive parents—felt that they knew best because they were older and thus did not have to listen to Dwayne. "I told my parents I don't want to do this anymore; I am going to quit," explained Dwayne. His parents were not happy about this decision, but Dwayne left his position anyway.

As his schedule opened up, he was able to focus more on school and learned about an organization his friend had founded called the St. Martin Youth Parliament. Its goal was to provide young individuals opportunities to develop their leadership and public speaking skills as well as work with the Parliament of the island. In 2013, Dwayne was invited to the organization after showing some interest. He joined it and fell in love with the experiences and opportunities it provided. He even decided to run for a leadership position in the organization. After giving a speech, Dwayne was elected and became a member of the leadership team.

After being in this organization for a year, he was invited to a major conference with government officials and leaders. Three people were elected to speak in front of the Royal Family of the Netherlands and other dignitaries in the region—and Dwayne was one of them. He was told he would be the third speaker. All of a sudden, the people running this conference changed the speaker order, and, at the last minute, Dwayne was called up to speak before he had even finished writing his speech! Dwayne stated, "I got called up, I delivered the first half of my speech, I improved the second half, and I got a standing ovation, even from the royal highness." He won "Best Presenter of the Day" even though he made up half of his speech on the fly! Dwayne is grateful for this experience because "if it wasn't for the friend who brought me to the Youth Parliament and the mentors in the organization, I would have never gotten the opportunity to speak in front of royalty."

This phenomenal presentation led to him being invited to the Governor's Symposium. And two months later, Dwayne was elected the president of the Youth Parliament. He worked with the Prime Minister of the Island as the youth representative to help create sustainable development on the island. He spoke with youth around the island to hear their input and what they wanted to see change in their communities. He continued to work with the government to create a plan that the younger generation approved of.

After all of these political experiences, Dwayne learned about the Watson Institute in Boulder, Colorado. At the time, they offered a degree in social entrepreneurship, which was a field of study that really intrigued him. He decided to apply, and he was accepted! In our interview, Dwayne said, "When I told my adoptive parents that I was going to Colorado to study, they didn't really support my vision." Time passed, and the program was about to start. All of the students were in Colorado, except for Dwayne, as he did not have money for a flight or tuition. This seemed like the end of his entrepreneurial road.

Out of the blue, one of the politicians Dwayne worked with reached out to him and asked him how he was doing. Dwayne explained his situation regarding the Watson Institute, and this politician offered to not only play for Dwayne's flight to Colorado but also offered to pay for the first half of his tuition. "If it weren't for the members in my network and the relationships I've developed, I don't think that [going to Colorado] would have happened."

In May of 2020, Dwayne graduated from this program with a bachelor's degree in Science and Social Entrepreneurship. He not only learned a great deal about entrepreneurship and changing the world, but he also "was able to develop a network of advisors and mentors." He was able to tap into his network when hosting a conference dedicated to supplying entrepreneurs on small islands. He was able to tap into his network to find free guest speakers to present to the 650 people who attended the conference.

Dwayne currently works in Washington, DC supporting young entrepreneurs by connecting them to mentors and advisors through an incubator program. In the future, Dwayne wants to continue building his network, as well as to develop a platform that allows entrepreneurs on small islands to connect with each other, access resources, and find funding/investors. "People really underestimate the power of the network," explained Dwayne, but he has learned firsthand how important a community is because of how much they have helped him achieve his goals.

*

TAKEAWAY

Research shows that 85 percent of work positions are filled through networking and genuine relationships. Such connections and support help you achieve your true potential no matter what you decide to do with your life. But the million-dollar question is: How do you find support and people to connect with? Countless numbers of books and articles outline networking and relationship-building strategies (and I encourage looking into some of them). But for the purpose of time, I have outlined a few tips to build professional relationships that have worked for me and may work for you.

1. Let them talk about themselves

Researchers from Harvard University have found people love talking about themselves (Tamir and Mitchell 2012). I am sure this does not come as a surprise to most of you, considering that humans spend 30 to 40 percent of their speech output talking about themselves. This does not mean you should let the other person dominate the conversation—you should talk about yourself as well—but it does mean allowing others to speak about themselves brings them joy and may help with the relationship. It is something to keep in mind.

2. Make a good first impression

Princeton University found it only takes one hundred milliseconds to register a first impression (Lebowitz 2018). This does not mean if you screw up the first time, the relationship is a bust, but it does mean starting off on the right foot helps. Show you care by being prepared and dressing nicely. You don't need to wear designer clothes; instead, show you put time into your appearance, and you value the other person's time.

3. Be genuine

No one likes a "user" or someone who takes advantage of other people. Build a relationship to build a relationship and not to get something out of the other person. Be genuine with your approach and help them, if you can, add value to their lives. It is just as important to support others as it is to receive support.

4. Don't be shy

Obviously, this is easier said than done because many people are naturally introverts. However, it is essential to remember there are many people and communities out there who are willing to support you. Worst-case scenario: they say no. So I encourage you to go out and meet new people, attend conferences, and connect with people online.

Finding a support network may seem like a lot of work, and it is, but the benefits make your efforts worthwhile. Television producer Michael Schur put it best when he said, "You can't achieve anything entirely by yourself. There's a support system that is a basic requirement of human existence. To be happy and successful on earth, you just have to have people that you rely on."

CONCLUSION

Yay! You finished the book! It may not have been easy to get through all of these pages, but you owe yourself a pat on the back for pushing through. That being said, your journey should not end here. All of the words in this book serve as advice, which can be implemented into your life.

While reading and learning are the more manageable parts (they are not necessarily easy, but they are certainly *easier*), applying this knowledge to the real world might be a little more complicated. While I sincerely hope you enjoyed this book, the blunt reality is this: it was not worth the read if you are not going to do anything with the knowledge you gained.

Think of it as learning to cook a new dish. Say you watched a bunch of videos, read some cookbooks, and even took a few lessons from a professional chef. If you never actually cook the dish or do anything with the ability to cook, how beneficial is that skill?

Entrepreneurship and business are not different. Learning is one thing, but applying is another. Two people may read the same book, and it may change their lives in completely different ways. An ample reason for this is likely that one person actually used the book in their life while the other simply read and then promptly forgot about it.

I am not saying you need to change the course of your life entirely, nor am I declaring that you need to do everything this book recommends. Rather, I am suggesting that you take at least one lesson from it and see how it can improve your life. Baby steps—that is my one ask.

SUMMARY
- It is critical to limit doubt so that you can move forward with little hesitation

- You will encounter setbacks, but you must move on

- Failure is a learning opportunity

- Trying new things is important for success and growth

- Having a genuine purpose is key

- Be a lifetime learner

- Don't make everything perfect; rather, take action

- Starting young is the best route to take, don't wait.

- Having a support network is key

You have learned so much and have a wealth of potential. But, that potential will only be unlocked if you actually apply such lessons to life.

Go forth, and best of luck!

ACKNOWLEDGMENTS

Thank you to everyone who supported me in this journey—emotionally and financially. This would not have been possible without you!

Alphabetical by Last Name

Karla Alcabes
Edasnice Alec
Laura Armenio
Neha Bar
Angeli Breen
David Bufton
Diane Carlson
Aditya Desai
Nimesh Gandhi
Ruchira Garg
Dwayne Griffith
Lopa Gupta
Rajiv Gupta
Surina Gupta
Hannah Harbaugh
Rahsaan Holley
Vedavyas Jampanaboyana
Jenny Jilla
Alexa Kayman
Eric Koester
Andy Li
Alexandre Masmejean

Ben Mathew	Tayo Rockson
Malekai Mischke	Satvik Sethi
Hemanshu Nigam	Narendra Shah
Ashley Olafsen	Neepa Shah
Roopa Parekh	Teju Shah
Atisha Patel	Daniel Sigal
Joe Philbin	Siddarth Sridhar
Sydney Phillips	Brennan Stark
Rajendra Prasad	Smita Tilak
Amy Rind	Tatarit Yensuang
Marc Rind	Sanjay Zaveri

APPENDIX

INTRODUCTION

"Quote by Norman Vincent Peale." *Goodreads*. https://www.goodreads.com/quotes/4324-shoot-for-the-moon-even-if-you-miss-you-ll-land.

Simovic, Dragomir. "39 Entrepreneur Statistics You Need to Know in 2021." *smallbizgenius* (blog). May 27, 2021. https://www.smallbizgenius.net/by-the-numbers/entrepreneur-statistics/#gref.

DOUBT

Alton, Larry. "Why Low Self-Esteem May Be Hurting You at Work." *NBC News*, Nov. 15, 2017. https://www.nbcnews.com/better/business/why-low-self-esteem-may-be-hurting-your-career-ncna814156.

Ingraham, Christopher. "America's Top Fears: Public Speaking, Heights and Bugs." *Washington Post*. Oct. 30, 2014. https://www.washingtonpost.com/news/wonk/wp/2014/10/30/clowns-are-twice-as-scary-to-democrats-as-they-are-to-republicans/.

Marano, Hara Estroff. "Our Brain's Negative Bias." *Psychology Today*, June 20, 2003. https://www.psychologytoday.com/us/articles/200306/our-brains-negative-bias.

"Quote by Henry Ford." *Goodreads*. https://www.goodreads.com/quotes/978-whether-you-think-you-can-or-you-think-you-can-t--you-re.

Warrell, Margie. "Is Negativity Bias Sabotaging Your Success?" *Forbes*, Sept. 30, 2017. https://www.forbes.com/sites/margiewarrell/2017/09/30/combat-negativity-bias/?sh=33055d7234a8.

BAD THINGS WILL HAPPEN

"10 Ways to Become More Resilient." *Nottingham City Council.* http://www.nottinghamchildrenspartnership.co.uk/media/370469/10-ways-to-become-more-resilient.pdf. Accessed June 29, 2021.

Agarwal, Pragya. "Here Is Why Grit Is So Important for Entrepreneurs." *Forbes*, Feb. 17, 2019. https://www.forbes.com/sites/pragyaagarwaleurope/2019/02/17/here-is-why-grit-is-so-important-for-entrepreneurs/?sh=681f82a251dd.

Bazelais, Paul, David John Lemay, and Tenzin Doleck. "How Does Grit Impact College Students' Academic Achievement in Science?" *European Journal of Science and Mathematics Education* 4, no. 1 (2016): 33–43. https://files.eric.ed.gov/fulltext/EJ1107756.pdf.

Custer, George A. "It's Not How Many Times You Get Knocked Down That Count, It's How Many Times You Get Back Up." *Passiton.* https://www.passiton.com/inspirational-quotes/3274-its-not-how-many-times-you-get-knocked-down.

Ellin, Abby. "Special Report: Why Developing Resilience May Be the Most Important Thing You Can Do for Your Well-Being Right Now." *Everyday Health.* Last modified December 17, 2020. https://www.everydayhealth.com/wellness/state-of-resilience/.

Fessler, Leah. "'You're No Genius': Her Father's Shutdowns Made Angela Duckworth a World Expert on Grit." *Quartz at Work*, Mar. 26, 2018. https://qz.com/work/1233940/angela-duckworth-explains-grit-is-the-key-to-success-and-self-confidence/.

Folkman, Joseph. "New Research: 7 Ways to Become a More Resilient Leader." *Forbes*, Apr. 6, 2017. https://www.forbes.com/sites/joefolkman/2017/04/06/new-research-7-ways-to-become-a-more-resilient-leader/?sh=67a173087a0c.

Gomes, Craig. "Facing Obstacles as an Entrepreneur." *Craig Gomes* (blog). Medium. Mar. 30, 2019. https://medium.com/@gomescraig/starting-a-business-is-like-running-an-obstacle-race-3e42024f5311.

Rosen, Amy. "Why 'Grit' May Be Everything for Success." *Entrepreneur*, Aug. 7, 2015. https://www.entrepreneur.com/article/247840.

FAILURE IS NOT A TOTAL FAIL

Bryant, Sean. "How Many Startups Fail and Why?" *Investopedia*, Nov. 9, 2020. https://www.investopedia.com/articles/personal-finance/040915/how-many-startups-fail-and-why.asp.

Demers, Jayson. "51 Quotes to Inspire Success in Your Life and Business." *Inc.* Nov. 3, 2014. https://www.inc.com/jayson-demers/51-quotes-to-inspire-success-in-your-life-and-business.html.

Hendricks, Drew. "How the 25 Richest Americans Failed Miserably." *Inc.* July 14, 2014. https://www.inc.com/drew-hendricks/how-the-top-25-richest-americans-failed-before-during-or-after-they-made-million.html.

Koraza, Toni. "The Importance of Failure in Every Success." *Start it up* (blog). Medium. Mar. 12, 2019. https://medium.com/swlh/the-importance-of-failure-in-every-success-15af9195892.

"Nigel Barber Ph.D." *Psychology Today*. https://www.psychologytoday.com/us/contributors/nigel-barber-phd. Accessed June 29, 2021.

Patel, Deep. "6 Proven Strategies to Rebound from Failure." *Entrepreneur*, Nov. 28, 2016. https://www.entrepreneur.com/article/285244.

Ruth, Angela. "Thomas Edison - 10,000 Ways That Won't Work." *Due* (blog). Last modified August 22, 2016. https://due.com/blog/thomas-edison-10000-ways-that-wont-work/.

TRY NEW THINGS

Alton, Larry. "A Look at the Incredible Benefits of Trying New Things." *HuffPost*. May 15, 2017. https://www.huffpost.com/entry/a-look-at-the-incredible-benefits-of-trying-new-things_b_59196b49e4b02d6199b2f129.

"Biography of Gabrielle Jordan." Breaking Barriers: Aetna African American Calendar. https://breakingbarriers.aetna.com/assets/bios/43-Breaking-Barriers-Gabrielle-Jordan.pdf. Accessed June 19, 2021.

Cornell University. "Ed Helms' 2014 Cornell Convocation Speech." May 25, 2014. 28:09. https://www.youtube.com/watch?v=CPnAnRsqiao.

Deane, Michael T. "Top 6 Reasons New Businesses Fail." *Investopedia*. Last modified February 28, 2020. https://www.investopedia.com/financial-edge/1010/top-6-reasons-new-businesses-fail.aspx.

Gabrielle Jordan. "How Gabrielle Jordan Went from Local Designer to TLC's 'Kid Tycoons' Reality Show." Feb. 18, 2017. 5:11. https://www.youtube.com/watch?v=VF9c3R5MDrQ.

Gregoire, Carolyn. "6 Reasons to Step Outside Your Comfort Zone." *HuffPost*. Sept. 26, 2014. https://www.huffpost.com/entry/stepping-outside-your-comfort-zone_n_5872638.

" H. Jackson Brown, Jr. Quotes." *Brainy Quote*. https://www.brainyquote.com/quotes/h_jackson_brown_jr_379375.

Henry, Alan, and Rebecca Fishbein. "The Science of Breaking Out of Your Comfort Zone (and Why You Should)." *lifehacker* (blog). Sept. 26, 2019. https://lifehacker.com/the-science-of-breaking-out-of-your-comfort-zone-and-w-656426705.

Logothetis, Leon. "5 Ways to Move Outside Your Comfort Zone." *HuffPost*. Last modified January 11, 2018. https://www.huffpost.com/entry/5-ways-to-move-outside-yo_b_14086232.

Pallud, Alizée. "Entrepreneurship: Why Trying New Things Is Good for You." *Alizée Pallud* (blog). Medium. Mar. 6, 2018. https://medium.com/@alizeepallud/entrepreneurship-why-trying-new-things-is-good-for-you-7eab2b981937.

Stillman, Jessica. "Science Has Just Confirmed That If You're Not Outside Your Comfort Zone, You're Not Learning." *Inc.* Aug. 14, 2018. https://www.inc.com/jessica-stillman/want-to-learn-faster-make-your-life-more-unpredictable.html.

TEDx Talks. "The Making of a Young Entrepreneur: Gabrielle Jordan Williams at TEDxRockCreekPark." May 11, 2013. 5:27. https://www.youtube.com/watch?v=EblQj_pZFlQ.

POWER OF PURPOSE

Aziz, Afdhel. "The Power of Purpose: The Business Case for Purpose (All the Data You Were Looking for Pt 1)." *Forbes*, Mar. 7, 2020. https://www.forbes.com/sites/afdhelaziz/2020/03/07/the-power-of-purpose-the-business-case-for-purpose-all-the-data-you-were-looking-for-pt-1/?sh=360858a030ba.

Conner, Cheryl. "The Secret to Success in Business: Focus on Impact." *Forbes*, June. 3, 2015. https://www.forbes.com/sites/cherylsnappconner/2015/06/03/the-secret-to-success-in-business-focus-on-impact/?sh=283496d71ca3.

Constable, Kimanzi. "3 Reasons Why Focusing on Impact Instead of Income Makes You More Money Sooner." *Entrepreneur*, Nov. 17, 2014. https://www.entrepreneur.com/article/239540.

Kleckner, Joe. "39 Awe-Inspiring Quotes from Simon Sinek." *Addicted2Success*. Aug. 14, 2017. https://addicted2success.com/quotes/39-awe-inspiring-quotes-from-simon-sinek/.

Robinson, Lisa. "Why Chance the Rapper Makes Music for Free (and How He Actually Makes Money)." *Vanity Fair*, Feb. 9, 2017. https://www.vanityfair.com/hollywood/2017/02/why-chance-the-rapper-music-is-free-and-how-he-makes-money.

Weisul, Kimberly. "Bombas: Charitable at the Start, Profitable by Year 3, and Only 3 Employees Have Ever Quit." *Inc.* June, 2019. https://www.inc.com/magazine/201906/kimberly-weisul/bombas-socks-low-turnover-emergency-fund-best-workplaces-2019.html.

ALWAYS LEARN

"55 Inspirational Quotes About Learning." *Growth Engineering* (blog). Sept. 1, 2020. https://www.growthengineering.co.uk/55-quotes-about-learning/.

Coleman, John. "Lifelong Learning Is Good for Your Health, Your Wallet, and Your Social Life." *Harvard Business Review*, Feb. 7, 2017. https://hbr.org/2017/02/lifelong-learning-is-good-for-your-health-your-wallet-and-your-social-life.

"Mark Cuban." *Biography*. Last modified September 1, 2020. https://www.biography.com/business-figure/mark-cuban.

Newman, Nic. "'Give a Man a Fish...' Why Successful Entrepreneurs Are Lifelong Learners (and How to Become One)." *NAXN* (blog). Medium. Oct. 31, 2017. https://medium.com/@naxn/give-a-man-a-fish-why-successful-entrepreneurs-are-lifelong-learners-and-how-to-become-one-do1bb1c3791.

Powell, Gerry E. "Reference to 'Teaching a Man to Fish' Isn't from Bible." *CantonRep*. Last modified September 12, 2010. https://www.cantonrep.com/article/20100912/news/309129902.

St. Louis Teens. "Mark Cuban Gives Advice to Teen Entrepreneurs." July 29, 2020. 20:18. https://www.youtube.com/watch?v=NEsJoBdDvg8.

Stillman, Jessica. "Reading 30 Minutes a Week Can Make You Happier and Healthier." *Inc.* Aug. 3, 2015. https://www.inc.com/jessica-stillman/30-minutes-a-week-can-make-you-happier-and-healthier.html.

Tank, Aytekin. "Why Continuous Learning Is Critical for Entrepreneurs and Their Teams." *Entrepreneur*, May 8, 2019. https://www.entrepreneur.com/article/331900.

Winerman, Lea. "By the Numbers: Lifelong Learning." *American Psychological Association* 48, no. 2 (Winter 2017): 80. https://www.apa.org/monitor/2017/02/numbers.

TAKING ACTION AND EXECUTING

BigSpeak Speakers Bureau. "Kim Perell - How to Execute and Make Things Happen." Oct. 5, 2018. 13:50. https://www.youtube.com/watch?v=DHgHMvbVxig.

Blanco, Octavio. "After a Painful Bankruptcy She Created a Multimillion Dollar Marketing Firm." *CNN*. Aug. 19, 2016. https://money.cnn.com/2016/08/19/news/economy/kim-perell-amobee.

Chen, James. "Analysis Paralysis." *Investopedia*. Last modified June 19, 2021. https://www.investopedia.com/terms/a/analysisparalysis.asp.

Forleo, Marie. "Self-Made Millionaire: The Simple Strategy That Helped Increase My Odds of Success by 42%." *CNBC*. Last modified September 13, 2019.
https://www.cnbc.com/2019/09/13/self-made-millionaire-how-to-increase-your-odds-of-success-by-42-percent-marie-forleo.html.

Kane, Becky. "The Science of Analysis Paralysis." *ambition & balance* (blog).
https://blog.doist.com/analysis-paralysis-productivity/.

Keuilian, Bedros. "Why Indecision Is Costing You Money, Time and Opportunity." *Entrepreneur*, Oct. 16, 2019.
https://www.entrepreneur.com/article/340376.

Kleckner, Joe. "21 Chris Sacca Quotes on Life & Business." *Addicted2Success* (blog). Jan. 12, 2018.
https://addicted2success.com/quotes/21-chris-sacca-quotes-on-life-business/.

"Quote by Anthony Robbins." *Goodreads*.
https://www.goodreads.com/quotes/877199-the-only-impossible-journey-is-the-one-you-never-begin.

Ries, Julia. "Here's What Happens to Your Body When You Overthink." *HuffPost*. Last modified February 6, 2020.
https://www.huffpost.com/entry/overthinking-effects_l_5dd2bd67e4b0d2e79f90fe1b.

Tank, Aytekin. "Escape Your Head: How Overthinking Is Hurting Your Business." *Entrepreneur*, July 8, 2020.
https://www.entrepreneur.com/article/352597.

TEDx Talks. "The Secret to Success: It's Not What You Think | Kim Perell | TEDxPepperdineUniversity." Dec. 16, 2019. 13:31.
https://www.youtube.com/watch?v=SRI1jWcUgKA.

THE BEST TIME TO START IS NOW

"5 Reasons to Start a Business in Your 20s and 30s." *Entrepreneur*, May 12, 2016.
https://www.entrepreneur.com/article/275314.

"7 Ways Entrepreneurship Helps You Be a Better...Anything." *Entrepreneur*, Mar. 20, 2017.
https://www.entrepreneur.com/article/290269.

DeMatteo, Megan. "The Average American Has $90,460 in Debt—Here's How Much Debt Americans Have at Every Age." *CNBC*. June 9, 2021.
https://www.cnbc.com/select/average-american-debt-by-age/.

Haste & Hustle. "Jesse Kay: Business Is for Teenagers Too!" Apr. 4, 2018. 9:20.
https://www.youtube.com/watch?v=TBQ5cr_vjIU.

MUNPlanet. "'What Are the Benefits of Being a Young Entrepreneur?" *MUNPlanet* (blog). Medium. June 19, 2017.
https://medium.com/munplanet/what-are-the-benefits-of-being-a-young-entrepreneur-ef1be8d4c819.

Press Release PR Newswire. "'20 Under 20s' 19-Year-Old Founder, Jesse Kay, to Launch 'Trendsetters' a New Podcast Focusing on Interviews with World Class Entrepreneurs, Athletes, Politicians and Entertainers." *Markets Insider.* Aug. 26, 2019. https://markets.businessinsider.com/news/stocks/20-under-20s-19-year-old-founder-jesse-kay-to-launch-trendsetters-a-new-podcast-focusing-on-interviews-with-world-class-entrepreneurs-athletes-politicians-and-entertainers-1028473646.

"Procrastination Quotes." *Goodreads.*
https://www.goodreads.com/quotes/tag/procrastination.

Ronzio, Chris. "4 Real Reasons You Should Start a Business While You're Young." *Inc.* June 4, 2018.
https://www.inc.com/chris-ronzio/4-real-reasons-you-should-start-a-business-while-youre-young.html.

TEDx Talks. "True Confessions of a Tie-coon | Shreyas Parab | TEDxYouth@IndependenceSchool." Apr. 18, 2016. 5:22.
https://www.youtube.com/watch?v=9pvkJEtPz3E.

Twin, Alexandra. "Risk Tolerance." *Investopedia.* Last modified October 29, 2020.
https://www.investopedia.com/terms/r/risktolerance.asp.

"Why the Young Learn More Easily." *BBC.* Last modified November 23, 2006.
http://news.bbc.co.uk/2/hi/health/6172048.stm.

THE IMPORTANCE OF COMMUNITY

Bonnell, Michael. "We Become What We Surround Ourselves With." *Michael Bonnell* (blog). Medium. Jan. 23, 2019.
https://medium.com/@michaeljosephbonnell/we-become-what-we-surround-ourselves-with-f953a290b940.

Lebowitz, Shana. "15 Proven Ways to Get People to Take You Seriously." *Insider.* May 21, 2018.
https://www.businessinsider.com/how-to-get-people-to-take-you-seriously-2018-5.

Morin, Amy. "5 Reasons Studies Say You Have to Choose Your Friends Wisely." *Psychology Today, April 10, 2015.*
https://www.psychologytoday.com/us/blog/what-mentally-strong-people-dont-do/201504/5-reasons-studies-say-you-have-choose-your-friends.

Park, William. "How Your Friends Change Your Habits - for Better and Worse." *BBC.* May 20, 2019.
https://www.bbc.com/future/article/20190520-how-your-friends-change-your-habits---for-better-and-worse.

Tamir, Diana I, and Jason P. Mitchell. "Disclosing Information About the Self Is Intrinsically Rewarding." *Proceedings of the National Academy of Sciences* 109, no. 21 (Spring 2012): 8038–8043. DOI: 10.1073/pnas.1202129109.

"Top 25 Support Systems Quotes." *AZQuotes.*
https://www.azquotes.com/quotes/topics/support-systems.html.

van Doorn, Maarten. "'You Are the Average of the Five People You Spend the Most Time With." *Maarten van Doorn* (blog). Medium. June 20, 2018. https://medium.com/the-polymath-project/you-are-the-average-of-the-five-people-you-spend-the-most-time-with-a2ea32d08c72.

Vukova, Christina. "73+ Surprising Networking Statistics to Boost Your Career." *Review 42*. Last modified June 28, 2021. https://review42.com/resources/networking-statistics/.

www.ingramcontent.com/pod-product-compliance
Lightning Source LLC
LaVergne TN
LVHW011831060526
838200LV00053B/3972